AMERICAN MISCELLANY

MICHAEL A. COUSIN

While all information contained in this book has been researched by the author and is believed by him to be factual, errors may occur. The author is not responsible for any inaccuracies, omissions, or discrepancies.

If you have found an error, notice an oversight or would like to make a comment you can email the author at Michael@AmericanMiscellany.com.

Thanks to my wife Stephanie, who puts up with me every day.

For my Mom,
who taught me to never stop learning.

CROSSING THE BORDER

There are 24 legal border crossings to Mexico from the United States. From West to East they are:

San Ysidro, California / Tijuana, Baja California

Otay Mesa, California / Tijuana, Baja California

Calexico, California / Mexicali, Baja California

Andrade, California / Algondones, Baja California

San Luis, Arizona / San Luis Rio Colorado, Sonora

Lukeville, Arizona / Sonoyta, Sonora

Sasabe, Arizona / El Sásabe, Sonora

Nogales, Arizona / Nogales, Sonora

Naco, Arizona / Naco, Sonora

Douglas, Arizona / Agua Prieta, Sonora

Columbus-Border City, New Mexico / Puerto Palomas, Chihuahua

Santa Teresa, New Mexico / San Jerónimo, Chihuahua

El Paso, Texas / Ciudad Juárez, Chihuahua

Presidio, Texas / Ojinaga, Chihuahua

Del Rio, Texas / Ciudad Acuña, Coahuila

Eagle Pass, Texas / Piedras Negras, Coahuila

Laredo, Texas / Nuevo Laredo, Tamaulipas

Roma, Texas / Ciudad Miguel Alemán, Tamaulipas

Rio Grande City, Texas / Camargo, Tamaulipas

Los Ebanos, Texas / Ciudad Gustavo Díaz Ordaz, Tamaulipas

Pharr, Texas / Reynosa, Tamaulipas

Progreso, Texas / Nuevo Progreso, Tamaulipas

Los Indios, Texas / Matamoros, Tamaulipas

Brownsville, Texas / Matamoros, Tamaulipas

Useful Maori

Kia-ora – Hi/Thank you (informal)
Tena koe – Hello (one person)
Tena korua – Hello (two people)
Tena kotou – Hello (three or more people)
Kei te pahea koe (korua/kotou) – How are you doing?
Kei (Korua/Kotou) te pai. - I am (We are) fine.
pakeha – A light skinned person usually of European decent.
kai - food
hoa - friend
Haere mai - Come here.
No hea koe? - Where are you from?
Excuse me. - Aroha mai.
Goodbye (informal)/See you again - Ka kite ano.
Goodbye (to someone leaving) - Haere ra.
Goodbye (to someone staying) - E noho ra.

Your Cheese Has Holes in it.

In North America "Swiss Cheese" is a type of cheese otherwise known as Swiss Emmental. Most types have a distinctive appearance, it has holes in it. The holes are formed because of the bacteria used to make the cheese and the temperature that the cheese is aged at. While the cheese is aging the propioni bacteria consume the lactic acid in the milk-base and produce acetate, propionic acid and carbon dioxide gas. The carbon dioxide produces bubbles in the cheese that make the holes (known as 'eyes') that we know and love. The acetate and propionic acid give Swiss Cheese its distinct flavor. Swiss Cheese without holes is called 'blind.'

Advertising Jingles

OSCAR MEYER WEINERS - "I wish I were an Oscar Meyer Weiner" Start with the classics. These 60's jingles for Oscar Meyer are so effective and beloved that they are still used over 40 years after they were first produced. You can't beat the original animation that went along with them, plus you can hear the second verse that very few know.

OSCAR MEYER BOLOGNA - "My Bologna Has a First Name..." Another Oscar Meyer classic that I'm sure already has you humming and spelling. This is the only reason the last two generations of Americans have been able to spell bologna.

MENTOS - "The Freshmaker" This song and commercial were parodied so many times it is known in some form to just about every American. The Foo Fighters parodied the commercials in their music video for "Big Me."

DOUBLEMINT GUM - "Double Your Pleasure, Double Your Fun" This commercial featured twins and identical dogs nothing like twins talking at the same time to sell gum.

McDONALD'S - "You Deserve a Break Today" is incorrectly attributed to Barry Manilow, though he did sing it for one of the commercials. It was actually written by Kenny Karen, a jingle singer/songwriter. The jingle and variations of it have been used since the 1970's.

CHILI'S - "I want my Baby Back Ribs" This is probably one of the most iconic jingles in the last 20 years. It has been voted one of the most likely jingles to get stuck in your head by AdAge. In fact, if you are over 30 you probably already have "I want my baby back, baby back baby back..." going in your head. You're welcome.

Semaphore Flags

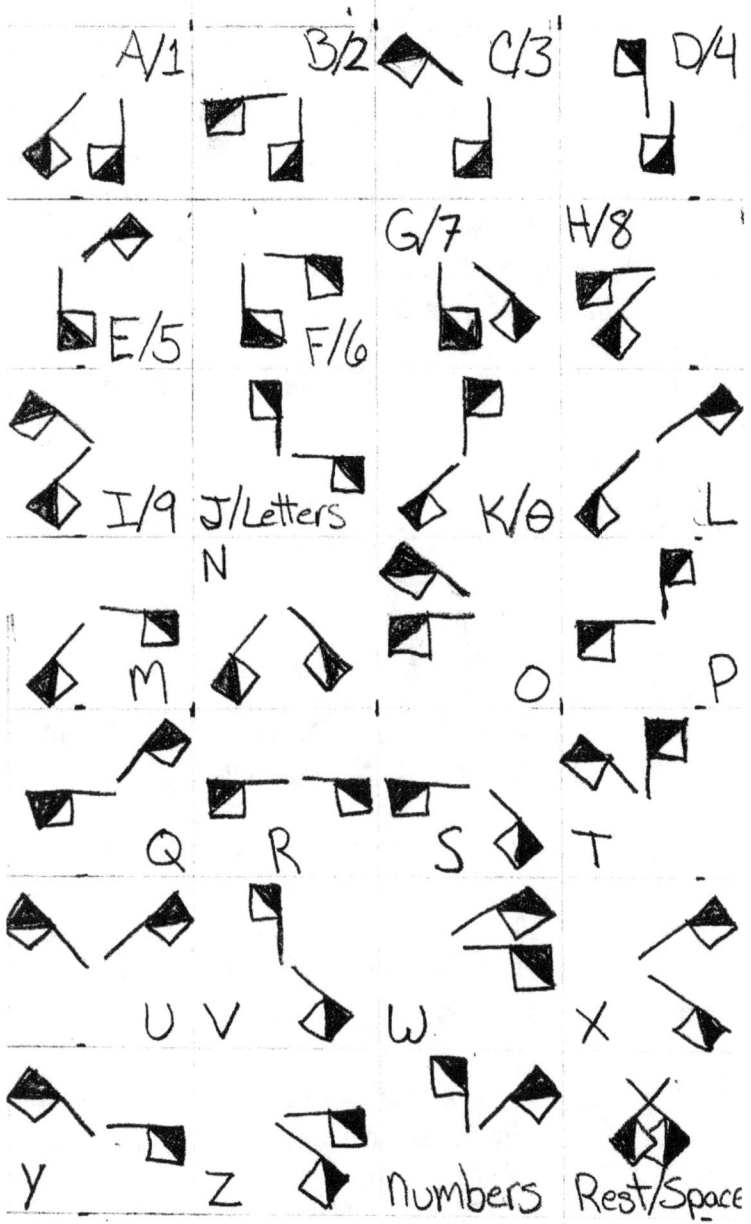

AMERICAN COINS

There are six different denominations of coins currently minted by the US Mint. Both Half Dollar and Dollar coins are not commonly used, but are readily available at banks and some businesses. In the past 10 years there have been special commemorative series designs on Quarters, Nickels, Pennies and Dollar Coins. The Mint also produces various proofs, commemorative coins and medals, which are available for sale as collector's pieces.

ONE CENT (PENNY) - Copper Plated Zinc, 2.5g, 0.75 in. diameter, 1.55mm thick, plain edge.

FIVE CENTS (NICKEL) - Cupro-Nickel, 5.0g, 0.835 in. diameter, 1.95mm thick, plain edge.

ONE DIME (10¢) - Cupro-Nickel, 2.268g, 0.705 in. diameter, 1.35mm thick, 118 reeded edge.

QUARTER DOLLAR (25¢) - Cupro-Nickel, 5.67g, 0.955 in. diameter, 1.75mm thick, 119 reeded edge.

HALF DOLLAR (50¢) - Cupro-Nickel, 11.34g, 1.205 in. diameter, 2.15mm thick, 150 reeded edge.

ONE DOLLAR ($1) - Manganese-Brass, 8.1g, 1.043 in. diameter, 2.0mm thick, lettered edge.

The US Mint produces other commemorative coins and proof sets, but they are not necesarily legal tender that can actually be used in commerce.

Sand Dunes in Alaska?

Alaska is home to 25 square miles (65km^2) of sand dunes. Though usually associated with warm beaches and hot deserts near the equator, the Great Kobuk Sand Dunes are located North of the Arctic Circle. Temperatures can reach 100°F (38°C) in the summer. The dunes are the largest active sand dunes in the arctic.

Poor Richard

Benjamin Franklin began publishing "Poor Richard's Almanack" in 1732 as a way to supplement his printing business in Philadelphia. The almanac was very popular throughout the colonies and became one of the most widely read publications in America. Many of the popular sayings that Franklin penned as Richard Saunders are still recognized by Americans today. They include many phrases that are so common, most people don't even know where they come from.

The Whole Nine Yards

The phrase "to give it the whole nine yards," meaning to give something all your effort or everything you have, comes from Word War II. WWII Era fighters had .50 caliber machine guns mounted on the wings. These machine guns were fed by ammunition that was loaded on belts the were fed through the gun rapidly as it fired. The fighters held 27 feet of ammo, or nine yards (3 feet = 1 yard). If you fired all of your ammo during a mission you gave it, "the whole nine yards."

The Smithsonian Institution

The Smithsonian Institution, located in Washington, DC, is the world's largest museum complex. It consists of 19 museums, 9 research centers and the National Zoo. It was named after James Smithson, a British scientist who stated in his will that if his nephew (his heir) should die without heirs that his estate should go "to the United States of America, to found at Washington, under the name of the Smithsonian Institution, an establishment for the increase and diffusion of knowledge among men." The Smithsonian has been doing that for nearly 200 years. Here are the museums and buildings that are part of the Smithsonian Institute.

African American History and Culture
African Art Museum
Air and Space Museum
Air and Space Museum Udvar-Hazy Center
American Art Museum
American History Museum
American Indian Museum
American Indian Museum Heye Center
Anacostia Community Museum
Arts & Industries Building
Cooper-Hewitt, National Design Museum
Freer Gallery
Hirshorn Museum and Sculpture Garden
National Zoo
Natural History Museum
Portriat Gallery
Postal Museum
Renwick Gallery
Sackler Gallery

Smithsonian Institution Building (the castle)

Smithsonian Research Centers

Archives of American Art
Conservation Biology Institute (SCBI)
Environmental Research Center (SERC)
Harvard-Smithsonian Center for Astrophysics
Smithsonian Archives
Smithsonian Libraries
Marin Station at Fort Pierce
Museum Conservation Institute (MCI)
Tropical Research Institute (STRI)

Tickle the Ivories

On a standard Piano there are 88 keys, 52 white and 36 black. The number is arrived at because the instrument covers about 7 octaves. Each octave contains 8 white keys and 5 black keys. That means that there should be 91 keys, right? Well, those 7 octaves actually share note "C" at the top and bottom of corresponding octaves, so that takes us down to 85 if you take out the 6 duplicates. Where are the extra 3 keys? All the way to the left of the keyboard are the extra "A", "B" and "B♭" that are there to round out the 88. These notes are included because they are basically the same range as the human voice (give or take).

Golf Balls

A standard golf ball has 336 dimples in it. During an average tee-off on the PGA tour the ball reaches a speed of about 160 mph.

MAP OF CENTRAL PARK, NYC

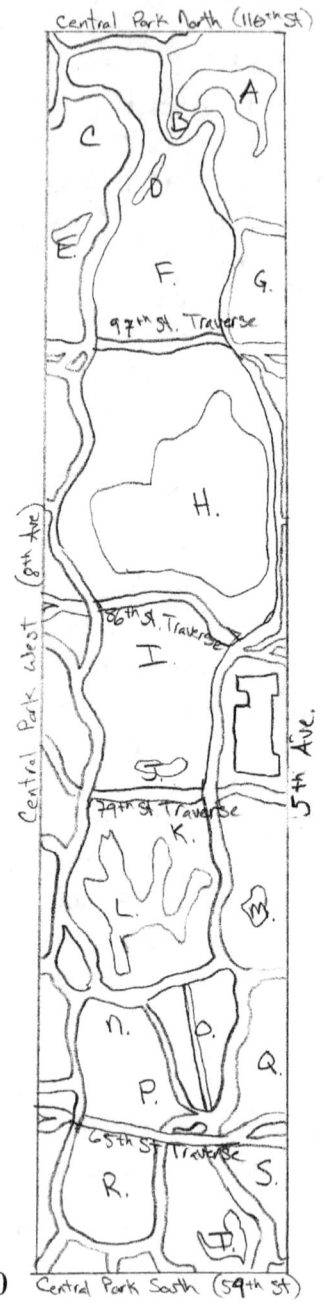

A. Harlem Meer

B. Lasker Rink/Pool

C. The Great Hill

D. The Loch

E. The Pool

F. North Meadow

G. East Meadow

H. Jacqueline Kennedy
Onassis Reservoir

I. The Great Lawn

J. Turtle Pond

K. The Ramble

L. The Lake

M. Conservatory Water

N. Bowling Greens

O. The Mall

P. Sheep Meadow

Q. East Green

R. Heckscher Playground

S. Central Park Zoo

T. The Pond

Military Salutes

In the US Navy, Marine Corps, and Coast Guard hand salutes are only given outdoors and when a cover (a hat or helmet) is worn. The Army and Air Force give salutes both covered and uncovered, but saluting indoors is not proper except when formally reporting to a superior officer or during an indoor ceremony.

In combat situations hand salutes are generally forbidden, as enemy snipers may use them to identify officers.

The US Navy adopted the British 21-gun solute as the standard salute for heads of state. Over the years fewer rounds came to signify salutes for lower ranking officers and dignitaries. Today ground based artillery batteries also follow this same pattern for salutes.

Commander-In-Chief - 21-guns
5 star officers - 19-guns
4 star officers - 17-guns
3 star officers - 15-guns
2 star officers - 13-guns
1 star officers - 11-guns

Three-volley salutes are rendered during military funerals in the US, usually by a rifle party of seven. Even though the total shots fired is 21 and it is commonly referred to as a "21-gun salute" technically 21-gun salutes are only fired by artillery batteries or naval vessels.

During the civil war the bugle call "Taps" was used in place of the three-volley salute due to the proximity of the enemy. Today they are both part of military rights performed at funerals.

The Supreme Court of the United States

The Supreme Court of the United States is the only part of the Judicial Branch of government explicitly created by the Constitution. There are currently 9 members of the Supreme Court, 8 Associate Justices and the Chief Justice. Associate Justices and the Chief Justice are appointed by the President of the United States and confirmed by the Senate for life, though they may retire at their discretion.

A Term of the Supreme Court begins on the first Monday in October. The Court normally alternates between 'sitting' and being 'in recess' every two weeks during the term. When 'sitting' the court hears cases from 10am to 3pm, with oral arguments being limited to 30 minutes for each side. The court may hear up to 24 cases in one 'sitting.'

When the Court is in session the Justices are announced by the Marshal. All rise at the sound of the gavel and remain standing until the Justices are seated. The Marshall announces: "The Honorable, the Chief Justice and the Associate Justices of the Supreme Court of the United States. Oyez! Oyez! Oyez! All persons having business before the Honorable, the Supreme Court of the United States, are admonished to draw near and give their attention, for the Court is now sitting. God save the United States and this Honorable Court!"

The Court only sits to announce orders and opinions in May and June and recesses at the end of June. During the rest of the summer and early fall the Justices consider motions and applications and make preparations for cases scheduled for the next term.

Notable Nebraskans

Fred Astaire - dancer/actor. Born in Omaha.

Marlon Brando - actor. Born in Omaha.

Warren Buffett - investor/businessman. Born & lives in Omaha.

Gerald Rudolph Ford - 38th President of the US. Born in Omaha.

Frank W. Leahy - Notre Dame football coach. Born in O'Neill.

Malcolm X - civil rights activist. Born in Omaha.

Red Cloud - Oglala Sioux Chief. Born in North Platte.

Dick Cheney - former Vice President. Born in Lincoln.

Lawrence R. Klein - winner of Nobel Prize in Economics. Born in Omaha.

Val L. Fitch - Winner of the Nobel Prize in Physics. Born in Marriman.

Johnny Carson - Host of *The Tonight Show*. Born in Corning, raised in Norfolk.

Joseph "Bob" Kerrey - 35th Governor of Nebraska, former US Senator, Medal of Honor recipient.

Fictional Nebraskans

The Wizard of Oz - In the books by L. Frank Baum. In the 1939 film he claims to be from Kansas.

Scott Summers - Cyclops from the X-Men comic book series spent most of his childhood in an orphanage in Omaha.

Penny - The main female character (played by Kaley Cuoco) on the TV sitcom *The Big Bang Theory* hails from Omaha.

The Works of Edgar Allen Poe

Short Stories

"The Black Cat"

"The Cask of Amontillado"

"A Descent into the Maelstrom"

"The Facts in the Case of M. Valdemar"

"The Fall of the House of Usher"

"The Gold-Bug"

"Ligeia"

"The Masque of the Red Death"

"The Murders in the Rue Morgue"

"The Oval Portrait"

"The Pit and the Pendulum"

"The Premature Burial"

"The System of Doctor Tarr and Professor Fether"

"The Tell-Tale Heart"

Poems

"Al-Araaf"

"Annabel Lee"

"The Bells"

"The City in the Sea"

"The Conqueror Worm"

"A Dream Within a Dream"

"Eldorado"

"Eulalie"

"The Haunted Palace"

"To Helen"

"Lenore"

"Tamerlane"

"The Raven"

"Ulalume"

Other Works

Politian - His only play.

The Narrative of Arthur Gordon Pym of Nantucket - His only complete novel.

Football and Rivalry

Football and rivalries go back a long time. They are especially prominent among high school and college teams. The following is a list of the oldest college rivalries by division as well as the first year the two teams met on the gridiron.

Football Bowl Subdivision: Minnesota-Wisconsin (1890)

Football Championship Subdivision: Lafayette-Lehigh (1884)

Division II: Emporia St.-Washburn (1899)

Division III: Williams-Amherst (1881)

Top of the mornin' to ya!

The correct response to the traditional Irish greeting, "Top of the mornin' to ya" is "and the rest of the day to yourself."

UPC Barcodes

The Universal Product Code is a type of barcode used to track products and scan them at point-of-sale locations. The system is widely used in the United States, Canada, United Kingdom, Australia, New Zealand and other countries. UPC-A is the most common form consisting of two groups of numbers. The first is the manufacturer's identification number and the second group is the individual product number. The number of digits available give a theoretical maximum of 1 Trillion numbers (1,000,000,000,000).

Scottish Inventors

ARTHUR JAMES ARNOT(1865-1946), inventor of the electric drill

ALEXANDER BAIN(1811-1877), inventor of the electric clock

ALEXANDER GRAHAM BELL(1847-1922), inventor of the telephone

JAMES BLYTH(1839-1906), inventor of the electricity producing wind turbine

DAVID BUICK(1854-1929), inventor of the overhead valve engine, founder of the Buick Motor Company

JAMES CHALMERS(1782-1853), inventor of the adhesive postage stamp

SIR DUGALD CLARK(1854-1932), inventor of the two-stroke internal combustion engine

THOMAS CAUGHTRIE(1917-2008), inventor of locking pliers or vise-grips

ROBERT DAVIDSON(1804-1894), inventor of the electric locomotive

SIR JAMES DEWAR(1842-1923), inventor of the thermos

JOHN BOYD DUNLOP(1840-1921), inventor of pneumatic or inflatable tires, founder of Dunlop Tires

JAMES GOODFELLOW(1937-), inventor of the ATM and PIN numbers

JOHN SCOTT HALDANE(1860-1936), inventor of the gas mask

WILLIAM THOMSON, LORD KELVIN(1824-1907), inventor of the Kelvin temperature scale

JAMES LEE(1831-1904), inventor of the detachable rifle magazine and the bolt action

JOHN LOUDON MCADAM(1756-1836), invented the process for building roads with a smooth, hard surface binding stones together with tar, hence the term "tarmac"

CHARLES MACINTOSH(1766-1843), inventor of waterproof fabrics for use in raincoats

JOHN NAPIER(1550-1617), inventor of logarithms

DR. SIR JAMES YOUNG SIMPSON(1811-1870), discoverer of the anesthetic properties of chloroform

CHARLES TENNANT(1768-1838), inventor of chlorine bleach

ROBERT WATSON-WATT(1892-1973), inventor of radar

The Sun is a Mass of Incandescent Gas

The Sun is made of plasma, mostly hydrogen and helium. Plasma is a state of matter (like solid, liquid, and gas) that happens when matter is super-heated. About 74% of the Sun's mass is Hydrogen and about 24% is Helium. The remaining 2% is made of trace elements such as Oxygen, Iron, Silicon, Carbon, Nickel and other elements.

Many students have learned about the Sun through the song "Why Does the Sun Shine?" written by Tom Glazer in the 1950's. It was famously covered by the band They Might Be Giants in 1993 with a much more upbeat tempo.

Giraffe Tongues

Giraffe's have a tongue that is about 20 inches long. The purple-black prehensile appendage is used to pull foliage to its mouth and groom its head. It's even long enough to clean its own ears!

Pucker Up

In France a "French Kiss" is known as a *baiser amoureux* (Lover's Kiss) or a *baiser florentin* (Florentine Kiss). It became known as a French Kiss in English speaking areas in the early 20th Century when it was widely believed that the French were much more liberal about such practices.

Tongue Twisters

Peter Piper picked a peck of pickled peppers.
Did Peter Piper pick a peck of pickled peppers?
If Peter Piper picked a peck of pickled peppers,
where's the peck of pickled peppers Peter Piper picked?

Betty Botter had some butter,
"But," she said, "this butter's bitter.
If I bake this bitter butter,
it would make my batter bitter.
But a bit of better butter--
that would make my batter better."

So she bought a bit of butter,
better than her bitter butter,
and she baked it in her batter,
and the batter was not bitter.
So 'twas better Betty Botter
bought a bit of better butter.

Mr. See owned a saw.
And Mr. Soar owned a seesaw.
Now See's saw sawed Soar's seesaw
Before Soar saw See,
Which made Soar sore.
Had Soar seen See's saw
Before See sawed Soar's seesaw,
See's saw would not have sawed
Soar's seesaw.
So See's saw sawed Soar's seesaw.
But it was sad to see Soar so sore
Just because See's saw sawed
Soar's seesaw!

Newborn Reflexes

A baby has several natural reflexes that tell you that their brain is developing normally. Reflexes are spontaneous and happen normally. Pediatricians usually check for the presence of these reflexes during an exam.

Root reflex: When the corner of the baby's mouth is touched the baby will turn in that direction and open their mouth.

Suck reflex: After rooting, sucking is the next natural reflex. When the roof of the baby's mouth is touched they will begin sucking.

Moro reflex: This is also known as a startle reflex. When startled by a loud sound or sudden movement the baby will throw their head back and extend their arms and legs, then pull their arms and legs back in. Only lasts about 5 or 6 months.

Tonic neck reflex: When the baby's head is turned to one side they will extend the arm on that side and the opposite arm will bend up at the elbow. Lasts 6 to 7 months after birth.

Grasp reflex: Stroking the palm of the hand will cause the baby to close their fingers. Only lasts a few months and is stronger in premature babies.

Babinski reflex: When you stroke the bottom of the foot firmly the baby's big toe will point up and the other toes will fan out. Lasts about 2 years.

Step reflex: When held upright on a solid surface the baby will pick up their foot and appear to take a step.

Super Bowl Champions

The Super Bowl started as the World Championship Game between the champions of the National Football League and the American Football League. The two leagues combined to form the new National Football League, becoming the National Football Conference, and the American Football Conference respectively. Super Bowls are traditionally numbered in Roman Numerals, are played in late January or early February on a neutral field hosted by alternating conferences. The winner of the game is the NFL Champion and is awarded the Vince Lombardi Trophy and each team member received a ring commemorating the win.

I - 1967	Green Bay Packers
II - 1968	Green Bay Packers
III - 1969	New York Jets
IV - 1970	Kansas City Chiefs
V - 1971	Baltimore Colts
VI - 1972	Dallas Cowboys
VII - 1973	Miami Dolphins
VIII - 1974	Miami Dolphins
IX - 1975	Pittsburgh Steelers
X - 1976	Pittsburgh Steelers
XI - 1977	Oakland Raiders
XII - 1978	Dallas Cowboys
XIII - 1979	Pittsburgh Steelers
XIV - 1980	Pittsburgh Steelers
XV - 1981	Oakland Raiders
XVI - 1982	San Francisco 49ers
XVII - 1983	Washington Redskins
XVIII - 1984	Los Angeles Raiders
XIX - 1985	San Francisco 49ers

XX - 1986	Chicago Bears
XXI - 1987	New York Giants
XXII - 1988	Washington Redskins
XXIII - 1989	San Francisco 49ers
XXIV - 1990	San Francisco 49ers
XXV- 1991	New York Giants
XXVI - 1992	Washington Redskins
XXVII - 1993	Dallas Cowboys
XXVIII -1994	Dallas Cowboys
XXIX - 1995	San Francisco 49ers
XXX - 1996	Dallas Cowboys
XXXI - 1997	Green Bay Packers
XXXII - 1998	Denver Broncos
XXXIII - 1999	Denver Broncos
XXXIV - 2000	St. Louis Rams
XXXV - 2001	Baltimore Ravens
XXXVI - 2002	New England Patriots
XXXVII - 2003	Tampa Bay Buccaneers
XXXVIII - 2004	New England Patriots
XXXIX - 2005	New England Patriots
XL - 2006	Pittsburgh Steelers
XLI - 2007	Indianapolis Colts
XLII - 2008	New York Giants
XLIII - 2009	Pittsburgh Steelers
XLIV - 2010	New Orleans Saints
XLV - 2011	Green Bay Packers
XLVI - 2012	New York Giants
XLVII - 2013	Baltimore Ravens
XLVIII - 2014	Seattle Seahawks
XLIX - 2015	New England Patriots

THE WEIGHT OF PAPER

In the US paper industry, measurements of paper density and weight are based on traditional sheet sizes which vary with the type of paper. Paper is described by the weight of 1 ream (500 sheets) but to the standard size of that paper type. Today paper is often not even produced in these sizes, but the traditional weight is still used.

Type of paper	Size (in inches)
Bible	25 X 38
Blanks	22 X 38
Blotting	19 X 24
Bond	17 X 22
Book	25 X 38
Cover	20 X 26
Glassine	24 X 36
Gummed	25 X 38
Index	25.5 X 30.5
Ledger	17 X 22
Manifold	17 X 22
Manuscript	18 X 31
Mimeograph	17 X 22
Newsprint	24 X 36
Offset	25 X 38
Onionskin	17 X 22
Opaque	25 X 38
Poster	24 X 36
Tag	22.5 X 28.5
or	24 X 36
Text	25 X 38
Tissue	24 X 36
Vellum Bristol	22.5 X 28.5
Writing	17 X 22

How to Tie a Necktie

The necktie as we know it was first popularized during the Thirty-Years' War when they were worn by Croatian soldiers in French armies. The name for the necktie in French is from the name for Croatia, hence "cravate."

It wasn't until the industrial revolution that demand for neckwear that was easier to tie and would stay in place during the entire day was needed. Several advances in the construction of ties until we ended up with something more or less like we see today. Width, design and knot are all a matter of personal preference and change with various fashions. Here are three of the most common knots used today.

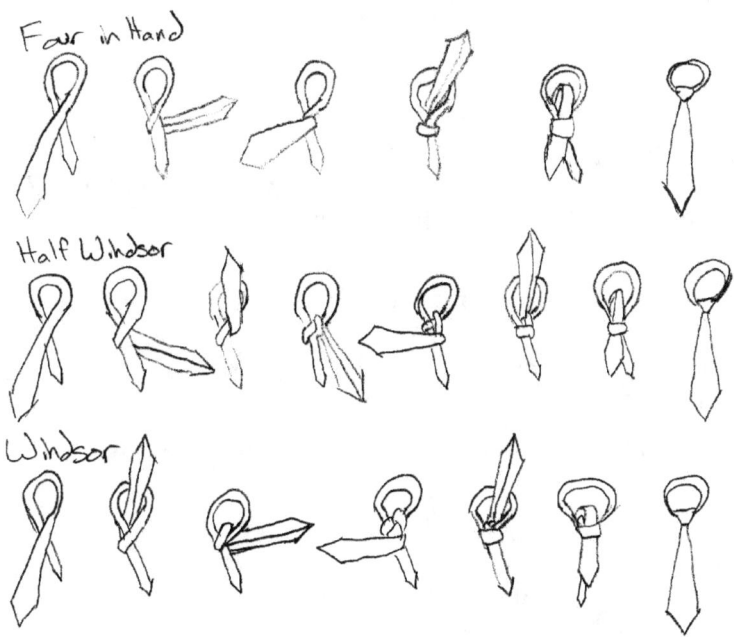

Radio and Television Call Signs

In general radio and television stations broadcasting in the United States are assigned a call sign beginning with W if located east of the Mississippi River and K if located west of the Mississippi River. There are several exceptions to this general rule that were established before this practice became standard such as KDKA in Pittsburgh and WACO in Waco, TX.

Everything You Know is Wrong

What we think we know changes over time. What was once accepted as true is shown to be plain wrong. As most scientific theories of the past have since been disproved, it is arguable that much of today's orthodoxy will also turn out, in due course, to be flawed. This is called "pessimistic induction."

'Merica

The US Navy currently has 19 aircraft carriers in service. That compares with 12 aircraft carriers currently in service with every other country in the world.

Fuzzy Wuzzy

The Grizzly Bear is the official state animal of California and appears on the state flag. No Grizzly Bears have been found in California since 1922.

Read It, Don't Eat It

There are actually more public libraries in the US than McDonald's Restaurants.

Idaho License Plates

Idaho licence plates have a 7 digit alpha-numeric number that is divided into two sections. The first 1, 2, or 3 digit letter or number-letter code indicates the county that issued the plate. The other 4, 5, or 6 digits are the plate number. Plate numbers are assigned numerically starting with 1, making the shortest licence plate numbers in the US possible in some counties (2 digits). Below are the county codes that represent each of the 44 counties of Idaho. These codes only appear on standard Idaho licence plates. There are over 30 varieties of licence plates issued by the Idaho Department of Transportation and each has a different numbering system.

County	Code	County	Code
Ada	1A	Gem	1G
Adams	2A	Gooding	2G
Bannock	1B	Idaho	I
Bear Lake	2B	Jefferson	1J
Benewah	3B	Jerome	2J
Bingham	4B	Kootenai	K
Blaine	5B	Latah	1L
Boise	6B	Lemhi	2L
Bonner	7B	Lewis	3L
Bonneville	8B	Lincoln	4L
Boundary	9B	Madison	1M
Butte	10B	Minidoka	2M
Camas	1C	Nez Pierce	N
Canyon	2C	Oneida	1O
Caribou	3C	Owyhee	2O
Cassia	4C	Payette	1P
Clark	5C	Power	2P
Clearwater	6C	Shoshone	S
Custer	7C	Teton	1T
Elmore	E	Twin Falls	2T
Franklin	1F	Valley	V
Fremont	2F	Washington	W

THE FIRST FLIGHT

Wilbur and Orville Wright of Dayton, OH were the first people to design, build, and fly a heavier than air flying machine. They flew their Wright Flyer 120 feet on December 17, 1903 at Kitty Hawk, NC. The aircraft that was piloted by Orville in that historic flight is now on display at the Smithsonian Institute's Air and Space Museum in Washington, DC.

Interestingly, a modern Boeing 747 has a wingspan of 212 ft. (64m), 92 ft. longer than that first flight.

MANHATTAN'S AREA CODE

New York City was given the area code 212 when area codes were first introduced in 1947. This was because it is the fastest code to dial from a rotary telephone (only 5 tones) and all telephones at the time were rotary. In North America area codes never begin with 1.

It is this same reason that Chicago's original area code is 312 and Los Angeles has 213. Today only the borough of Manhattan retains the 212 area code, though it is overlaid with several others. The outer boroughs of New York have been given their own area codes over time as well, making 10 digit dialing the norm in New York City.

HALF OF AMERICA

About half of all Americans live within 50 miles (80km) of their birthplace. About half (55%) live within 50 miles of a coastline and almost half of all Americans have an account on Facebook.com or MySpace.com.

What Do You Call That?

The plastic things on the end of shoelaces are called aglets.

The ball on top of a flagpole is called a truck.

The back of a sock is called the gore.

The top section of a staple is called the crown.

The top of a window frame is known as the lintel.

The round spring in a clothespin is a grinning hole.

A nail has two parts, the head and the shank.

The "and sign" or "&" is called an ampersand.

The star on the end of a cowboy's spur is a rowel.

The "at sign" or "@" is called a "commercial at" or an arroba.

The metal band that holds the eraser on a pencil is a ferrule.

The back side of a hammer (opposite the striking face) is called the peen.

The "pound sign" or "#" is called an octothorpe.

The metal hoop that holds up a lampshade is the harp.

California Missions

The Catholic Missions founded by Spanish Padres between 1769 and 1823 were the first non-native settlements in what became California. Most are named for Saints. Six of the missions were founded before the Declaration of Independence was signed and only the last was founded after Mexican independence in 1821.

San Diego de Alcalá July 16, 1769

San Carlos Borromeo de Carmelo June 3, 1770

San Antonio de Padua July 14, 1771

San Gabriel Arcángel September 8, 1771

San Luis Obispo de Tolosa September 1, 1772

San Francisco de Asís (Mission Dolores) June 26, 1776

San Juan Capistrano November 1, 1776

Santa Clara de Asís January 12, 1777

San Buenaventura March 31, 1782

Santa Barbara December 4, 1786

La Purísima Concepción December 8, 1787

Santa Cruz August 28, 1791

Nuestra Señora de la Soledad October 9, 1791

San José July 11, 1797

San Juan Bautista June 24, 1797

San Miguel Arcángel July 25, 1797

San Fernando Rey de España September 8, 1797

San Luis Rey de Francia June 13, 1798

Santa Inés September 17, 1804

San Rafael Arcángel December 14, 1817

San Francisco Solano July 4, 1823

Presidential Quotes

In the end, it's not the years in your life that count. It's the life in your years.　　–　Abraham Lincoln

Repetition does not transform a lie into a truth.
　　　　　　　　　　– Franklin D. Roosevelt

Freedom is the open window through which pours the sunlight of the human spirit and human dignity.
　　　　　　　　　　– Herbert Hoover

Whenever you do a thing, act as if all the world were watching.
　　　　　　　　　　– Thomas Jefferson

An honorable defeat is better than a dishonorable victory.
　　　　　　　　　　– Millard Fillmore

The only man who makes no mistake is the man who does nothing.
　　　　　　　　　　– Theodore Roosevelt

Few men have virtue to withstand the highest bidder.
　　　　　　　　　　– George Washington

In the time of darkest defeat, victory may be nearest.
　　　　　　　　　　– William McKinley

Peace is not absence of conflict, it is the ability to handle conflict by peaceful means.
　　　　　　　　　　– Ronald Reagan

U.S. National Holidays

New Year's Day - January 1
Birthday of Martin Luther King, Jr. - Third Monday in January.
Washington's Birthday(President's Day) - Second Monday in February.
Memorial Day - Last Monday in May.
Independence Day - July 4.
Labor Day - First Monday in September.
Columbus Day - Second Monday in October.
Veterans Day - November 11.
Thanksgiving Day - Fourth Thursday in November.
Christmas Day - December 25.

Throwing an Anchor Overboard

A fisherman is rowing a boat on a very small lake. He throws an anchor into the water. What happens to the water level of the lake? Does it rise, fall, or stay the same? We do have a clear answer to this one: if the anchor chain is long enough to rest the anchor on the bottom, the water level actually drops. The weight of the anchor while on the boat displaces a volume of water which has the same mass as the anchor. Water is less dense than the anchor, so when in the boat the anchor displaces more water than it does when it's on the bottom (when it displaces only its own volume). If the anchor chain is too short to reach the bottom, the anchor remains part of the boat/anchor system so the water level stays the same.

Governors of Wyoming

(1) Francis E. Warren(R)   October 11, 1890-November 24, 1890
(2) Amos W. Barber(R)   November 24, 1890-January 2, 1893
(3) John E. Osborne(D)   January 2, 1893-January 7, 1895
(4) William A. Richards(R)   January 7, 1895-January 2, 1899
(5) DeForest Richards(R)   January 2, 1899-April 28, 1903
(6) Fenimore Chatterton(R)   April 28, 1903-January 2, 1905
(7) Bryant B. Brooks (R)   January 2, 1905-January 2, 1911
(8) Joseph M. Carey(D)   January 2, 1911-January 4, 1915
(9) John B. Kendrick(D)   January 4, 1915-February 26, 1917
(10) Frank L. Houx(D)   February 26, 1917-January 6, 1919
(11) Robert D. Carey(R)   January 6, 1919-January 1, 1923
(12) William B. Ross(D)   January 1, 1923-October 2, 1924
(13) Frank E. Lucas(R)   October 2, 1924-January 5, 1925
(14) Nellie Tayloe Ross(D)*   January 5, 1925-January 3, 1927
(15) Frank C. Emerson(R)   January 3, 1927-February 18, 1931
(16) Alonzo M. Clark(R)   February 18, 1931-January 2, 1933
(17) Leslie A. Miller(D)   January 2, 1933-January 2, 1939
(18) Nels H. Smith(R)   January 2, 1939-January 4, 1943
(19) Lester C. Hunt(D)   January 4, 1943-January 3, 1949
(20) Arthur G. Crane(R)   January 3, 1949-January 1, 1951
(21) Frank A. Barrett(R)   January 1, 1951-January 3, 1953
(22) Clifford Joy Rogers(R)   January 3, 1953 -January 3, 1955
(23) Milward L. Simpson(R)   January 3, 1955-January 5, 1959
(24) John J. Hickey(D)   January 5, 1959-January 2, 1961
(25) Jack R. Gage(D)   January 2, 1961-January 7, 1963
(26) Clifford P. Hansen(R)   January 7, 1963-January 2, 1967
(27) Stanley K. Hathaway(R)   January 2, 1967-January 6, 1975
(28) Edgar J. Herschler(D)   January 6, 1975-January 5, 1987
(29) Mike Sullivan(D)   January 5, 1987-January 2, 1995
(30) Jim Geringer(R)   January 2, 1995-January 6, 2003
(31) Dave Freudenthal(D)   January 6, 2003-

* First female Governor of any state.

Goldfish

A goldfish is one of the most common pets in the United States. It is true that a goldfish will grow as large as its environment allows however goldfish do have long term memory, they simply do not have a long attention span. Also, if a goldfish is not exposed to ultraviolet light, such as natural sunlight, they will become paler in color and may even turn white. Goldfish also do not have a stomach and a group of goldfish are called a "troubling." The most common name for a pet goldfish in the US? "Jaws."

A #2 Pencil

The average wood pencil in the US is about seven inches long. That means it can draw a continuous line about 35 miles long.

Seven by Seven

There were seven sheep on Noah's Ark as well as other animals. Only unclean animals went in two by two.

Empty Tomb

The tomb of the Unknown Soldier from the Vietnam War is empty. For many years the body of 1LT Michael Joseph Blassie (1948-1972) was designated the Unknown Service Member from the Vietnam War. Blassie's family, however, were aware that evidence from the crash site suggested the body might be his. Having secured permission to test the theory, the remains of the Unknown Soldier were exhumed on May 14, 1998.

Blu-ray Disc, DVD, and Compact Disc

Blu-ray Discs and DVDs have the same physical dimensions as Compact Discs and the now defunct HD-DVD. All the formats are 120mm (4.7 in.) in diameter and 1.2mm (0.047 in.) thick. The difference is in the layers on the readable side of the disc and the laser used to read the data stored. Below is a few facts about each format.

Compact Disc
Released: 1982
Storage Capacity: up to 700MB (about 80 minutes audio)
Read Laser: 780 nm wavelength, infrared and red edge
Primary Use: audio recordings, data

DVD
Released: 1995
Storage Capacity: up to 4.7GB single-layered, 8.7GB double-layered
Read Laser: 650 nm, infrared and red edge
Primary Use: video recordings, data

Blu-ray Disc
Released: 2006
Storage Capacity: up to 25GB per layer (2-3 layers are common)
Read Laser: 405 nm, "blue" (actually in the violet range)
Primary Use: high-definition video recordings, data

Dalmatians and Firefighters

The energetic, spotted dog associated with firefighters in the US comes by the job very honestly. Dalmatians originated in an area known as Dalmatia, in modern-day Croatia. Originally they are believed to have been guard dogs and bird dogs, but they really gained their fame as a carriage dog. They would run along a carriage and help direct the horses, especially in crowded cities where there was a lot of traffic. When fire engines were pulled by large horses, the Dalmatian's job was to lead the horses through the city streets so they could reach the fire as quickly as possible, then they would heard the horses a safe distance from the fire. Even though they are no longer needed to work the horses, firefighters still often keep a Dalmatian as a mascot and a companion.

Multiple Letters

There are few words in the English language that have a letter repeated more than twice in a row, mostly old spellings or rarely used words. Words such as godessship and duchessship have triple letters, though most today prefer a hyphenated spelling. The word esssse is the only native English word to have a quadruple letter. It is an obsolete word that has been replaced by a much simpler form, ashes.

Lobster Sizes

Maine lobster are marketed as: Jumbo (more than 2 lb), large (1.5 to 2 lbs), quarter (1.25-1.5 lbs), chicken (1 lb), & chix (less than 1 lb).

Penguins

Penguins are only found in the southern Hemisphere, with nearly 20 different species. The smallest is the Blue Penguin, found in New Zealand and Australia, that only grows to about 16 inches tall (43 cm). The largest is the Emperor Penguin found only in Antarctica which grows to a height of up to 4 feet tall (1.2 m). Some penguins are known to be able to jump up to 6 feet (1.8 m) in the air, yet penguins do not have knees.

The Liberty Bell

The Liberty Bell has a special place in the hearts of many Americans for its place in the tower of Independence Hall, but did you know that in the inscription on the bell it says, "By Order of the Assembly of the Province of Pensylvania for the State House in Philada." Notice that Pennsylvania is spelled wrong on the bell. Really it isn't spelled wrong, as standard spelling had not yet been adopted. In the US Constitution the new state is also referred to as "Pensylvania." The current spelling of Pennsylvania was not universally adopted until the 19th Century.

Storage Capacity of The Human Brain

In computer terms, it is estimated that the human brain can store over 4 terabytes of data (4000 gigabytes). That's the equivalent to about 8,000 hours of CD quality music, or about a terabyte less than all of Wikipedia's raw data as of 2010.

Starlight, Star Bright

Of all the stars in the sky, these are the 26 that are closest to our Sun. The name of the star is followed by its approximate distance in light-years.

1	Proxima Centauri (4.24 ly)
2	α Centauri A* (4.37 ly)
2	α Centauri B* (4.37 ly)
4	Barnard's Star (5.96 ly)
5	Wolf 359 (7.78 ly)
6	Lalande 21185 (8.29 ly)
7	Sirius A* (8.58 ly)
7	Sirius B (8.58 ly)
9	Luyten 726-8 A (8.73 ly)
9	Luyten 726-8 B (8.73 ly)
11	Ross 154 (9.68 ly)
12	Ross 248 (10.32 ly)
13	Epsilon Eridani* (10.52 ly)
14	Lacaille 9352 (10.74 ly)
15	Ross 128 (10.92 ly)
16	EZ Aquarii A (11.27 ly)
16	EZ Aquarii B (11.27 ly)
16	EZ Aquarii C (11.27 ly)
19	Procyon A* (11.402 ly)
19	Procyon B (11.402 ly)
21	61 Cygni A* (11.403 ly)
21	61 Cygni B* (11.403 ly)
23	Struve 2398 A (11.53 ly)
23	Struve 2398 B (11.53 ly)
25	Groombridge 34 A (11.62 ly)
25	Groombridge 34 B (11.62 ly)

* visible to the naked eye

By Any Other Name

Many words that were supposedly "coined" by William Shakespeare were most likely already in use, at least forms of them. Often Shakespeare used words in new ways, or provided the first time that a word appeared in print even though it was probably in common usage. This list notes the word and, if necessary, the new way it was first seen in print in one of Shakespeare's works.

addiction
amazement (as a noun)
bedazzled
bedroom
belongings
bump
cold-blooded
critic
disgraceful
droplet
employer
eyeball
to gossip (as a verb)
howl
luggage (as a noun)
majestic (as an adjective)
mimic
obscene
published
puking
puppy-dog
roadway
uncomfortable
uneducated
watchdog
widowed (as an adjective)

LEAST AND MOST POPULOUS COUNTIES

The most populous county in the United States according to the US Census Bureau is Los Angeles County, California with a population of about 9.8 million. The least populous county is Loving County, Texas with a population of only 67.

LONGEST RULING ROYAL FAMILY

Japanese Emperors have been a part of the Yamato Dynasty for over 2600 years. The most recent Emperor, Akihito is the 125th Emperor. He became Emperor on the death of his father in 1989. His ancestor, Emperor Jimmu, is traditionally considered to be the first Emperor, ascending to the throne in about 660 B.C.

EPOCH

An Epoch is a geologic time period that is based on a series in layers of rock. While geologic time periods do not have a set length, an epoch is usually in the tens of millions of years. Epochs are divided into ages and they make up periods.

Currently we are living in the Holocene epoch of the Quaternary period of the Cenozoic era of the Phanerozoic eon.

Epoch should not be confused with "epic" which refers to a impressively great poem, usually following a hero's journey.

#1 TV Shows

Nielson Media Research began measuring television viewership in 1950. Since then many shows have been the highest rated for any given year. These shows have been #1 between 1950 and 2010.

Texaco Star Theater
Arthur Godfrey's Talent Scouts
I Love Lucy
The $64,000 Question
Gunsmoke
Wagon Train
The Beverly Hillbillies
Bonanza
The Andy Griffith Show
Rowan & Martin's Laugh-In
Marcus Welby, M.D.
All in the Family
Happy Days
Laverne & Shirley
Three's Company
60 Minutes
Dallas
Dynasty
The Cosby Show
Roseanne
Cheers
Home Improvement
Seinfeld
ER
Who Wants To Be A Millionaire?
Survivor
Friends
CSI: Crime Scene Investigation
American Idol

NOTABLE EAGLE SCOUTS

PETER AGRE, MD - professor and microbiologist, winner of the 2003 Nobel Prize in Chemistry.

NEIL ARMSTRONG - First Man to walk on the Moon.

WILLIE BANKS - Olympic athlete, former world-record holder in triple jump and long jump.

MICHAEL BLOOMBERG - Mayor of New York City

GUION "GUY" S. BLUFORD JR. - Retired US Air Force officer and astronaut; first African American in space.

BILL BRADLEY - Former professional basketball player, US Senator and presidential candidate.

STEPHEN BREYER - Associate Justice of the US Supreme Court.

WILLIAM C. DEVRIES, MD - Surgeon and educator; transplanted the first artificial heart.

MICHAEL DUKAKIS - Former Governor of Massachusetts and presidential candidate.

MIKE ENZI - US Senator from Wyoming.

THOMAS FOLEY - Former speak of the US House of Representatives and US Ambassador to Japan.

GERALD R. FORD - 38th President of the United States.

STEVE FOSSETT - Word-record holder; first to circumnavigate Earth solo in a balloon and an airplane.

MICHAEL KAHN - Acadamy Award-winning film editor.

JAMES A. LOVELL JR. - Former US Navy officer and Astronaut; Commander of Apollo 13.

J. WILLARD MARRIOTT JR. - Chairman and CEO of Marriott International.

GEORGE MEYER - Writer and producer of "The Simpsons".

MIKE ROWE - Host of "Dirty Jobs" and Ford spokesman.

STEVEN SPIELBERG - Academy Award-winning film director and producer.

Bones Around the Eye

There are seven bones that make up the orbital cavity of the human skull. Those bones are, the Frontal bone, the Lacrimal bone, the Ethmoid bone, the Zygomatic bone, the Maxillary bone, the Palatine bone and the Sphenoid bone.

Grizzly Bears

The Grizzly Bear is a North American Subspecies of the Brown Bear. They often have fur with white tips that give it a silver or grizzled look, which is where the name comes from. They are one of the largest land animals in North America, standing about 7 feet (2.1 m)tall and weighing up to 800 lbs (362 kg). They are also quick, with animals being clocked at speeds over 30 mph (48 kph).

Twin Beds? You got some 'splainin' to do!

Famously now, Ricky and Lucy slept in twin beds in I Love Lucy. The Flintstones was the first cartoon to show a couple sleeping in the same bed. Many think that this is the first time this was shown on television. After Little Ricky was born on the show, Ricky and Lucy actually shared a bed, long before Fred and Wilma came on television in 1960. The first live-action depiction of a couple sleeping in the same bed on television was on Mary Kay and Johnny, the very first Situation Comedy, in 1947. Unfortunately very few episodes of Mary Kay and Johnny survive as it was produced live and recording equipment was in its infancy.

ODE TO A SQUIRREL

Ben Franklin had a squirrel brought to England in 1771 for the daughters of an Anglican Bishop that he was boarding with. The squirrel, named Mungo, was a very popular pet until he was killed by a dog named Ranger the next year. He wrote the following epitaph for the animal in a letter to one of the girls.

Alas! poor Mungo!
Happy wert thou, hadst thou known
Thy own Felicity!
Remote from the fierce Bald-Eagle,
Tyrant of thy native Woods,
Though hadst nought to fear from his piercing Talons;
Nor from the murdering Gun Of the thoughtless Sportsman.
Safe in thy wired Castle,
Grimalkin never could annoy thee.
Daily wert thou fed with the choicest Viands
By the fair Hand Of an indulgent Mistress.
But, discontented, thou wouldst have more Freedom.
Too soon, alas! didst thou obtain it,
And, wandering, Fell by the merciless Fangs,
Of wanton, cruel Ranger.
Learn hence, ye who blindly wish more Liberty,
Whether Subjects, Sons, Squirrels or Daughters,
That apparent Restraint may be real protection
Yielding Peace, Plenty, and Security.

Here Skugg Lies
Snug As a Bug In a Rug.

Don't Clean Pearls with Vinegar

Pearls are made out of nacre, which is mostly calcium carbonate. When it is exposed to an acid like vinegar it causes a chemical reaction that produces carbon dioxide and dissolves the pearl. You can find out if a pearl is real by putting a drop of vinegar on it, if it fizzes it's real, but I'd wipe it off pretty quick. If you need to clean pearls, I'd stick to regular water.

Wooden Oscars?

It is widely rumored that during World War II Academy Awards were made of wood. This is incorrect. Due to a metal shortage they were actually made of painted plaster for 3 years during the war. After the war was over, recipients could exchange the plaster statuette for the standard, gold-plated variety.

The word 'checkmate'

The word checkmate comes from the Arabic term Shāh Māt, which means "the King is ambushed." It is commonly thought that it means "the King is dead" because the word meaning "dead" is māta.

Big Bills

Prior to 1929 US currency was bigger. Banknotes issued by the Federal Government was approximately 7.4218 x 3.125 in (189 x 79mm). All notes were changed to their current size of 6.14 x 2.61 (156 x 66.3mm) beginning with the Series of 1928.

ANGLO-SAXON RUNES

Below is my approximation of the Anglo-Saxon Futhorc or alphabet. This set of characters was not universal, some areas used more or less characters at different times. The Latin Alphabet replaced these characters by the 10th Century AD.

feoh-F   ur-U   þorn-TH   os-O   rad-R   cen-C

gyefu-Y   wynn-W   hægl-H   nyd-N   is-I   jear-J

eeoh-EO   peorð-P   eolh-X   sigel-S   tyr-T   beorc-B

eoh-E   man-M   lagu-L   ing-NG   œðel-Œ   dœy-D

ac-A   œsc-Æ   yr-Y   ear-EA   iar-IA   kalc-K

kalc-KK   gar-G   cweorð-QU   stan-ST

44

British and American Spelling

British / American
aeroplane / airplane
aluminium / aluminum
carburettor / carburetor
moustache / mustache
mum(my) / mom(my)
theatre / theater
litre / liter
metre / meter
colour / color
flavour / flavor
honour / honor
rumour / rumor
connexion / connection
inflexion / inflection
catalogue / catalog
enrolment / enrollment
fulfil / fulfill
liveable / livable
cheque / check
chilli / chili
kerb / curb
mould / mold
storey / story
tyre / tire
sceptic / skeptic
organise / organize
recognise / recognize
realise / realize

Not all these examples are exclusive. Some forms are used on both sides of the Atlantic. The most common usage is shown.

Naming Planets

Of all the planets in our solar system, Earth is the only one not named after a Roman god. The name Earth is Germanic in origin and comes from the Old English word "eorþe" and is related to other Germanic words meaning Earth, such as "aarde" (Dutch), "Erde" (German) and "jord" (Swedish). Originally the word only referred to land, but gradually it was applied to the entire planet as well. The word "Terra" which is sometimes used in English as another name for Earth, is just the Latin word of the same meaning. Latin based languages use variations of this word in an approximate manner.

...U...V...W...

The Letter "W" is actually a double "V." It became popular in English after the Norman Conquest in the 11th Century, replacing the runic letter wynn "ƿ." Ironically, the letter "U" didn't fully separate from the letter "V" until the 14th Century, so "double-U" was a letter before "U".

Ethiopian Time

Time in Ethiopia is counted differently from in many Western countries. The Ethiopian day is reckoned as beginning at 6 AM as opposed to 12 AM, concurrently with sunrise throughout the year. To convert between the Ethiopian clock and Western clocks, one must add (or subtract) 6 hours to the Western time. For example, 2 AM local Addis Ababa time is called "8 at night" in Ethiopia, while 8 PM is called "2 in the evening".

Los Angeles Subway System

The first line of the Los Angeles Subway opened in 1990 as an attempt to alleviate heavy traffic on the city's freeways. After numerous extension lines the system now consists of over 17 miles of underground track with an average weekday usage of about 150,000 people, well below that of cities like New York, Boston, or Washington, DC.

Common and Uncommon Fears

Aerophobia – Fear of flying
Glossophobia – Fear of public speaking
Acrophobia – Fear of heights
Nyctophobia – Fear of the dark
Necrophobia – Fear of death
Arachnophobia – Fear of spiders
Anthrophobia – Fear of flowers
Cynophobia – Fear of dogs
Coulrophobia – Fear of clowns
Alektorophobia – Fear of chickens
Anglophobia – Fear of England or English culture
Linonophobia – Fear of string
Hippopotomonstrosesquippedaliophobia – Fear of long words

Pass the Honey, Honey

Honey is one of the few foods that does not spoil. (Others being things like, salt, sugar and dried rice). In fact, archeologists have found pots of honey in Egyptian tombs that is thousands of years old, yet still edible. Now, if only they had some 3000 year old biscuits...

Rodeo Events

In professional rodeo, events fall into two categories; rough stock events and timed events.

The rough stock events are: Bareback Riding, Saddle Bronc Riding and Bull Riding.

The timed events are: Steer Wrestling, Tie Down Roping, Team Roping and Barrel Racing.

Global Peace Index

The Global Peace Index is a list compiled by the Institute for Economics and Peace in Sydney, Australia. Using figures from worldwide sources on a variety of issues ranging from military expenditures to crime rates, the Institute has ranked nations since 2007. Below is the top 10 most peaceful nations for 2010.

1 - New Zealand
2 - Iceland
3 - Japan
4 - Austria
5 - Norway
6 - Ireland
7 - Denmark
8 - Luxembourg
9 - Finland
10 - Sweden

The United States, Canada, and Mexico were ranked 85th, 14th, and 107th respectively.

WHERE IS THE BATHROOM?

Arguably the most important phrase to know in any language is "Where is the bathroom?" As a public service, several languages are provided here.

French - Où est la toilet?
Spanish - ¿Dónde está el baño?
German - Wo ist das Badezimmer?
Italian - Dove la stanza da bagno è?
Dutch - Waar is de badkamer?
Russian - Где - ванная? (Gde zdes' vannaya komnata)
Portuguese- Onde o banheiro é?
Norwegian- Hvor er badet ?
Japanese - 化粧室はどこですか (Keshō-shitsu wa
                dokodesu ka)
Chinese - (Mandarin) 厕所在哪里 (cèsuǒ zài nǎli?)
            (Cantonese) 廁所喺邊度呀 (chisó hái bīndouh a?)
Samoan - 'O fea le faleuila?
Zulu - Ikuphi idawa yokugezela?
Haitian Creole - Kote twalèt la?
Tagalog - Nasaan ang banyo?
Hindi - बाथरूम कहां है (Baatharuum kahaan hai)
Arabic - ('ayn al hamam) مامحلا نيأ
Czech - Kde jsou toalety?
Bulgarian - Къде е банята? (Kade e banyata?)
Navajo - Háadish yah anída'aldah góne'?
Cebuano - Hain sa kaligoanan?
Quechua - Maypin bañu?
Maori - Kei hea te kaukau?
Latin - UBI EST LATRINA
Bengali - যেখানে বাথরুম হয় (Yēkhānē bātharuma haẏa)
Javanese - where is jedhing

Library of Congress Cataloging

In the Library of Congress books are categorized by class, shown below. Each class is further divided into a subclass (another letter) and then into more specific subjects within the subclass represented by a 3 digit number which is sometimes broken down further with a decimal value. Then there is a further classification by the Author's last name, and finally the year in which the work was published.

A - General Works
B - Philosophy, Psychology, Religion
C - Auxiliary Sciences of History
D - World History and History of Europe, Asia, Africa, Australia, New Zealand, Etc.
E - History of the Americas
F - History of the Americas
G - Geography, Anthropology, Recreation
H - Social Sciences
J - Political Science
K - Law
L - Education
M - Music and Books on Music
N - Fine Arts
P - Language and Literature
Q - Science
R - Medicine
S - Agriculture
T - Technology
U - Military Science
V - Naval Science
Z - Bibliography, Library Science, Information Resources (General).

Some Alphabet Soup Agencies

A selection of government agencies founded as part of FDR's 'New Deal' in the 1930's.

CAA - Civil Aeronautics Authority (now Federal Aviation Administration), 1933
CCC - Civilian Conservation Corps, 1933
CWA - Civil Works Administration, 1933
EBA - Emergency Banking Act, 1933
FAP - Federal Art Project, part of WPA, 1935
FCA - Farm Credit Administration, 1933
FCC - Federal Communications Commission, 1934
FDIC - Federal Deposit Insurance Corporation, 1933
FERA - Federal Emergency Relief Administration, 1933
FHA - Federal Housing Administration, 1934
FSA - Farm Security Administration, 1935
FWA - Federal Works Agency, 1939
HOLC - Home Owners Loan Corporation, 1933
NIRA - National Industrial Recovery Act, 1933
NLRB - National Labor Relations Board, 1934
NRA - National Recovery Administration, 1933
OC - Office of Censorship, 1941
OWI - Office of War Information, 1942
PWA - Public Works Administration, 1933
RA - Resettlement Administration, 1935
REA - Rural Electrification Administration (now Rural Utilities Service), 1935
SEC - Securities and Exchange Commission, 1934
SSB - Social Security Board (now Social Security Administration), 1935
TVA - Tennessee Valley Authority, 1933
USHA - United States Housing Authority, 1937
WPA - Works Progress Administration, 1935

Why is Paper 8.5 x 11?

Standard paper sizes in the United States are a matter of tradition and it is not really documented how most standard sizes of loose-leaf paper came into use. The American system is officially used in only the US, Canada, the Philippines and Chile, though it is also in de facto usage in Mexico. The standard sizes are listed below.

Letter 8.5 x 11 in. (216 x 279mm)
Legal   8.5 x 14 in. (216 x 356mm)
Government Letter* 8 x 10.5 in.
Ledger/Tabloid* 11 x 17 in. (279 x 432mm)

*Government Letter was used by the US Federal Government from 1921-1982. This is also known as "school letter" and is still the standard size of notebook paper today.
*Ledger and Tabloid are the same size paper with a different orientation. Leger is portrait (11 x 17) and Tabloid is landscape (17 x 11).

Point Blank

In external ballistics, point-blank range is the distance between a firearm and a target of a given size such that the bullet in flight is expected to strike the target without adjusting the elevation of the firearm. In forensics and popular usage, point-blank range has come to mean extremely close range (i.e., target within about a meter (3 ft) of the muzzle at moment of discharge but not close enough to be an actual contact shot). Both definitions are considered correct.

Major Volcanic Eruptions since AD 1000

These are all major volcanic eruptions with a VEI (Volcanic Exclusivity Index) of 6 or above that have occurred since AD 1000. For comparison, the 1980 eruption of Mt. St. Helens in Washington was only a VEI 5.

Mt. Pinatubo, The Philippines, 15 June 1991
Novarupta, Alaska, 6 June 1912
Santa María, Guatemala, 24 October 1902
Mt. Tarawera, New Zealand, 10 June 1886
Krakatoa, Indonesia, 26-27 August 1883
Mt. Tambora, Indonesia, 10 April 1815
Grímsvötn, Iceland, 1783-1785
Long Island, Papua New Guinea, 1660
Kolumbo, Santorini, Greece, 27 September 1650
Huaynaputina, Peru, 19 February 1600
Billy Mitchell, Soloman Islands, 1580
Bárðarbunga, Iceland, 1477
Kuwae, Vanuatu, 1452-1453
Quilotoa, Ecuador, 1280

Careful, That Cheese is a Bit Sharp

The terms sharp and mild refer to the flavor of cheddar cheese. The sharper the cheddar, the more tangy and complex it will taste. Marianne Smukowski, who heads up safety and quality applications at the Wisconsin Center for Dairy Research, says the term sharp is a marketing phrase that doesn't coincide with any guidelines or grades within the U.S. dairy industry. She says sharp cheddar is simply an aged piece of cheese, probably six to nine months old, while extra-sharp cheddar is likely one-and-a-half to two years old.

Amps, Volts, Watts and Ohms

Electricity is measured in several ways. The basic units of electricity are voltage (V), current (I), and resistance (r). Voltage is measured in volts, current is measured in amps, and resistance is measured in ohms. These three are always in relation to each other. Current is always equal to voltage divided by resistance or $I=V/r$. If you compare electricity to plumbing; voltage is the water pressure, current is the rate of flow, and resistance is the size of the pipe.

Power is measured in watts (W). Power equals voltage multiplied by current or $W=VI$. A standard outlet in a home in the US has 120 volts of electricity. This means that your 60 watt light bulb is drawing 0.5 amps or $60W=120V \times 0.5I$. Since electricity is usually purchased by the kilowatt hour it means that you can run a 60 watt light bulb all the time (731 hours a month) and that will equal about 44kWh. Since electricity costs on average about 11 cents per kWh that will cost you about $4.84 a month. If you leave all the lights on in an average house all the time you can spend about $217.80 a month. Dad really wasn't crazy when he told you to turn off you bedroom light when you left.

Thrice

There only three multiplicative numbers in English, which tell you how many times something happens. They are once, twice, and thrice. 'Once' is most common, 'twice' is used about equally with 'two times' but thrice has fallen out of favor in modern times. Ironically, there aren't any more after that, you just have to say four times, five times, etc.

Elvis #1 Songs

"I Forgot To Remember To Forget" (1955)
"Heartbreak Hotel" (1956)
"I Want You, I Need You, I Love You" (1956)
"Houng Dog" (1956)
"Don't be Cruel" (1956)
"Love Me Tender" (1956)
"Too Much" (1957)
"All Shook Up (1957)
"(Let Me Be Your) Teddy Bear" (1957)
"Jailhouse Rock" (1957)
"Don't" (1958)
"Hard Headed Woman" (1958)
"A Big Hunk O' Love" (1959)
"Stuck on You" (1960)
"It's Now or Never" (1960)
"Are You Lonesome Tonight?" (1960)
"Surrender" (1961)
"Can't Help Falling in Love" (1961)
"Good Luck Charm" (1962)
"Return to Sender" (1962)
"Blue Christmas" (1964)
"Crying in the Chapel" (1965)
"(Such an) Easy Question" (1965)
"I'm Yours" (1965)
"In the Ghetto" (1969)
"Suspicious Minds" (1969)
"The Wonder of You" (1970)
"You Don't Have to Say You Love Me" (1970)
"Burning Love" (1972)
"My Boy" (1975)
"Moody Blue" (1975)
"Way Down" (1977)
"My Way" (1977)

Trucker Slang

Alligator - Blown tire, or part of a tire on the road.
Antler Alley - Deer crossing.
Back Door - Behind you.
Bear - Police.
Bear Trap - Radar trap.
Big Slab - Interstate highway.
Bumper Sticker - Car following too closely.
County Mounty - Local Sheriff.
City Kitty - City Police.
Clean Shot - Clear, road is free of police.
Cash Register - Toll booth.
Comic Book - Log book.
Bobtail - Truck without a trailer.
Brake Check - Traffic slowing or stopping.
Dry Box - A regular trailer without refrigeration, etc.
Flip Flop - To turn around or return
Four Wheeler - Car
Granny Lane - The slow lane (usually on the right)
Hammer Lane - Fast lane (usually to the left)
Left Coast - West coast
Meat Wagon - Ambulance
Motion Lotion - Diesel or gasoline
Parking Lot - Truck hauling cars
Sesame Street - Channel 19 on the CB
Salt Shaker - Snow plow/salt truck
Yard Stick - Mile Marker
Wiggle Wagon - Truck pulling 2 or more trailers.
10-4 - Yes, okay, copy that
10-20 - What is your location?
10-33 - Emergency.

Longest Place-Name in the World

There is a grassy hilltop in New Zealand that holds the honor of being the place with the longest place name in the world. In Maori it is known as Taumatawhaka-tangihangakoauauotamateaturipukakapikimaunga-horonukupokaiwhenuakitanatahu.

The meaning of this name is "The place where Tamatea, the man with big knees, the climber of mountains, known as land-swallower who travelled about, played his nose flute to his loved one."

Alligators and Crocodiles

The State of Florida is one of the few places in the world where you are likely to find crocodiles and alligators side by side. The key to telling them apart is the teeth. When their mouth is closed, crocodiles have protruding teeth on their lower jaw. When an alligator closes its mouth, the teeth fit into pockets in its upper jaw. You can also look at the shape of its head, alligators have shorter noses with a more U-shaped feel, while crocodiles have a longer, V-shaped snout. In a pinch (or trying to avoid one) it's probably a rule to avoid both as either animal can break a human bone with its bite.

The Biggest City

Juneau, Alaska holds the distinction of being the largest city in the US by land area. Officially it covers about 3000 square miles, larger than the State of Delaware.

CABINET SECRETARIES

The President currently appoints 15 people to their "Cabinet." These 15 people each head a corresponding Federal Department.

NAME - YEAR CREATED
Secretary of State - 1789
Secretary of Defense - 1947
Secretary of the Treasury - 1789
Attorney General - 1789
Secretary of the Interior - 1849
Secretary of Agriculture - 1889
Secretary of Commerce - 1913
Secretary of Labor - 1913
Secretary of Health and Human Services - 1979
Secretary of Housing and Urban Development - 1966
Secretary of Transportation - 1967
Secretary of Energy - 1977
Secretary of Education - 1979
Secretary of Veterans Affairs - 1989
Secretary of Homeland Security - 2003

FORMER CABINET SECRETARIES

Postmaster General 1829-1971
Secretary of War 1789-1947 *(absorbed as Secretary of the Army under the Secretary of Defense)*
Secretary of the Navy 1798-1947 *(absorbed under the Secretary of Defense)*
Secretary of Commerce and Labor 1903-1913 *(Split into separate Commerce and Labor secretaries)*
Secretary of Health, Education and Welfare 1953-1979 *(renamed Health and Human Services after creation of Department of Education)*

THE MUSIC STAFF

The STAFF is the five line base for determining pitch in a written piece.

LEDGER LINES add above or below the staff to show notes beyond its normal range.

The TREBLE OR G CLEF shows the position of *G above Middle C* on the second line.

The BASE OR F CLEF show the position of *F below Middle C* on the fourth line.

The TENOR OR C CLEF shows the position of Middle C on the staff. The third line here.

The DRUM OR NEUTRAL CLEF is used for non-pitched instruments like percussion.

The BRACE is used to connect multiple parts played by the same instrument (like the piano, harp or some pitched percussion)

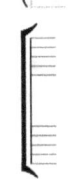

A BRACKET is used the join two parts played simultaneosly by different instruments (like choir parts or two violins, etc.)

The KEY SIGNATURE shows the series of sharps or flats that notes will take during the rest of the piece. Here is show *C Sharp Major* and *C Flat Major*.

A BAR LINE indicates the division of notes into measures, per the Time Signature.

A DOUBLE BAR LINE indicates the end of a section or a chage in Key or Time Signature.

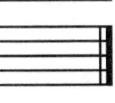

A BOLD DOUBLE BAR LINE indicates the end of a movement or the entire piece.

59

Canadian Prime Ministers

1st	Sir John A. Macdonald (Liberal-Conservative)	
	July 1, 1867-November 5, 1873	
2nd	Alexander Mackenzie (Liberal)	
	November 7, 1873-October 8, 1878	
-	Sir John A. Macdonald (Liberal-Conservative)	
	October 17, 1878-June 6, 1891**	
3rd	Sir John Abbott (Liberal-Conservative)	
	June 16, 1891-November 24, 1892	
4th	Sir John Thompson (Conservative)	
	December 5, 1892-December 12, 1894**	
5th	Sir Mackenzie Bowell (Conservative)	
	December 21, 1894-April 27, 1896	
6th	Sir Charles Tupper (Conservative)	
	May 1, 1896-July 8, 1896	
7th	Sir Wilfrid Laurier (Liberal)	
	July 11, 1896-October 6, 1911	
8th	Sir Robert Borden (Conservative)	
	October 10, 1911-October 12, 1917	
-	Sir Robert Borden (Unionist)	
	October 12, 1917-July 10, 1920	
9th	Arthur Meighen (N.L.C.)	
	July 10, 1920-December 29, 1921	
10th	William Lyon Mackenzie King (Liberal)	
	December 29, 1921-June 29, 1926	
-	Arthur Meighen (Conservative)	
	June 29, 1926-September 25, 1926	
-	William Lyon Mackenzie King (Liberal)	
	September 25, 1926-August 6, 1930	
11th	Richard Bedford Bennett (Conservative)	
	August 7, 1930-October 23, 1935	
-	William Lyon Mackenzie King (Liberal)	
	October 23, 1935-November 15, 1948	
12th	Louis St. Laurent (Liberal)	
	November 15, 1948-June 21, 1957	

13th	John Diefenbaker (Progressive Conservative)
	June 21, 1957-April 22, 1963
14th	Lester B. Pearson (Liberal)
	April 22, 1963-April 20, 1968
15th	Pierre Trudeau (Liberal)
	April 20, 1968-June 4, 1979
16th	Joe Clark (Progressive Conservative)
	June 4, 1979-March 3, 1980
-	Pierre Trudeau (Liberal)
	March 3, 1980-June 30, 1984
17th	John Turner (Liberal)
	June 30, 1984-September 17, 1984
18th	Brian Mulroney (Progressive Conservative)
	September 17, 1984-June 25, 1993
19th	Kim Campbell (Progressive Conservative)
	June 25, 1993-November 4, 1993
20th	Jean Chrétien (Liberal)
	November 4, 1993-December 12, 2003
21st	Paul Martin (Liberal)
	December 12, 2003-February 6, 2006
22nd	Stephen Harper (Conservative)
	February 6, 2006-November 4, 2015
23rd	Justin Trudeau (Liberal)
	November 4, 2015-

**Died in Office

Though not officially described in any document that is part of Canada's Constitution, the office of Prime Minister has been an important position since Confederation in 1867. The Prime Minister is not directly elected, but is usually the leader of the political party that has a majority in the Canadian House of Commons.

Prime Ministers are styled "The Right Honourable..." for life, (when referred to in the third person) but are referred to as "Mr. Prime Minister" in the first person only while in office.

Star Trek Movies

Title	Director
Star Trek: The Motion Picture	Robert Wise
Star Trek II: The Wrath of Khan	Nicholas Meyer
Star Trek III: The Search for Spock	Leonard Nimoy
Star Trek IV: The Voyage Home	Leonard Nimoy
Star Trek V: The Final Frontier	William Shatner
Star Trek VI: The Undiscovered Country	Nicholas Meyer
Star Trek: Generations	David Carson
Star Trek: First Contact	Jonathan Frakes
Star Trek: Insurrection	Jonathan Frakes
Star Trek: Nemesis	Stuart Baird
Star Trek	J. J. Abrams
Star Trek: Into Darkness	J. J. Abrams

What Kind of Number?

There are several kinds of numbers that are found in the English language. Ordinal numbers tell you the order that things are in (first, second, third, fourth...) Cardinal numbers tell you how many of something there are, (two, thirty-three, six, twelve...) and Nominal numbers are identifying numbers such as jersey numbers or telephone numbers.

Last Civil War Veteran

The last authenticated Civil War veteran was Albert Woolson of Minnesota. He was a young Union drummer boy in Company C, First Minnesota Volunteer Heavy Artillery from 1894-1895. He died, aged 109, in 1956. He served in the Civil War and lived to see the atomic bombs dropped on Japan.

USDA Grades

The United States Department of Agriculture inspects and grades beef and poultry that is to be sold in the US. Poultry has three grades, *Grade A, B,* and *C. Grade A* is the only one you are likely to see. *Grades B* and *C* are usually used in processed meats or sold without a grade. Beef is graded as *Prime, Choice, Select,* and *Standard* or *Commercial.* There are also *Utility, Cutter,* and *Canner* grades, but they are seldom, if ever, seen. They are primarily used for further processing.

Days of the Week

In English the days of the week are mostly based on old Germanic names that were translations of the Latin names for the week brought by Christianity.

Sunday - Literally "Sun's Day" from Germanic mythology associated with the sun goddess.
Monday - "Moon's Day" Most likely a translation from the Latin *dies lunae.*
Tuesday - "Tiw's Day" Named for Tiw the Norse god of single combat. Likely because of the Latin *dies Martis,* named for Mars, the Roman god of war.
Wednesday - "Woden's Day" for the Germanic god Woden (Odin in Norse mythology) a prominent god compared to the Roman god Mercury.
Thursday - "Thunor's Day" The Old English name for the Norse god Thor, god of thunder.
Friday - "Frige's Day" The Anglo-Saxon god Frige was roughly equivalent to the Roman goddess Venus.
Saturday - The only day of the week to have a Latin root in English. It literally means "Saturn's Day" for the Roman god Saturn.

63

Memorable Movie Lines

"Of all the gin joints in all the towns in all the world, she walks into mine." (Casablanca, 1942)

"I'll be back" (Terminator, 1984)

"Mama always said life was like a box of chocolates, you never know what you're gonna get." (Forest Gump, 1994)

"Frankly my dear, I don't give a damn." (Gone with the Wind, 1939)

"Badges? We ain't got no badges! We don't need no badges! I don't have to show you any stinking badges!" (The Treasure of the Sierra Madre, 1948)

"It's alive! It's alive!" (Dr. Frankenstein, Frankenstein, 1931)

"You've got to ask yourself one question: 'Do I feel lucky?' Well, do ya, punk?" (Dirty Harry, 1971)

"I'm going to make him an offer he can't refuse." (The Godfather, 1972)

"Toto, I've got a feeling we're not in Kansas anymore." (The Wizard of Oz, 1939)

"You're gonna need a bigger boat." (Jaws, 1975)

"I love the smell of napalm in the morning!" (Apocolypse Now, 1979)

"They call me Mister Tibbs!" (In the Heat of the Night, 1967)

"I have always depended on the kindness of strangers." (A Streetcar Named Desire, 1951)

"My precious." (The Lord of the Rings: The Two Towers, 2002)

SOME BINARY

0 = 0
1 = 1
2 = 10
3 = 11
4 = 100
5 = 101
6 = 110
7 = 111
8 = 1000
9 = 1001
10 = 1010
11 = 1011
12 = 1100
13 = 1101
14 = 1110
15 = 1111
16 = 10000
17 = 10001
18 = 10010
19 = 10011
20 = 10100
42 = 101010
100 = 1100100
254 = 11111110
255 = 11111111
1000 = 1111101000
2000 = 11111010000
2010 = 11111011010

GOLF

Until about 1848 most golf balls were made of leather tightly packed with feathers.

There are three golf balls on the moon, left by Alan Shepard during the Apollo 14 mission in 1971.

Until the mid 19th Century there was no set number of holes in a golf course. Each course could vary considerably in length and number of holes.

The oldest golf course in the world is the Old Links in Musselburgh, Scotland. It has been in use since 1672.

ISTANBUL NOT CONSTANTINOPLE

The modern city of Istanbul has been know by many names over its 2600 year history. It was known principally as Byzantium until the Third Century. By the Fourth Century it was known in the West as Constantinople, in honor of Constantine the Great. This was the most common name used for the city until the early 20th Century.

After the advent of the Republic of Turkey in 1923, the common Turkish name, Istanbul, became the name of choice. Istanbul is actually based on the Greek phrase meaning "in the City." In 1930, the Turkish Postal Service Law officially requested that foreigners refer to the city as Istanbul.

American - Metric Conversions

When people from other countries come to the United States it can be very difficult to convert common US measurements. Though based on the Imperial System of Britain, each unit is not necessarily equal to the Imperial unit of the same name.

1 inch= 2.54cm
1 foot (12 in.) = 30.48cm
1 yard (3 ft.) = 0.9144m
1 mile (1760 yd.) = 1.60934km

1 fluid ounce = 29.565mL
1 cup (8 fl. oz.) = 0.2366L
1 pint (2 cups) = 0.4732L
1 quart (2 pt.) = 0.9461L
1 gallon (4 qt.) = 3.7843L
1 oil barrel (42 gallons) = 158.99L

1 ounce= 28.35g
1 pound= 0.4536kg
1 ton= 0.9072 metric tonnes

Interstate Highway Specs

Interstate highway standards are defined by the American Association of State Highway and Transportation Officials. As of 2009 those standards are, in part:

Minimum of 2 lanes in each direction
Minimum lane width of 12ft (3.6m)
Minimum shoulder width of 10ft (3.0m)
Minimum inside shoulder width 4ft (1.2m)
Minimum median width of 36ft (11m)
Maximum grade of 6%
Minimum vertical clearance 16ft (4.9m)

State Demonyms

A demonym is the name for a person from a certain locality. In the US 'American' is usually the demonym of choice when speaking internationally, but within the states people are usually classified by state.

Sometimes it is common knowledge what you call a person from a particular state. In some states demonyms are attached to state run university mascots, or other historical or geographical features of the area.

Alabama = Alabaman, Alabamian
Alaska = Alaskan
Arizona = Arizonan
Arkansas = Arkansan
California = Californian
Colorado = Coloradan, Coloradoan
Connecticut = Connecticuter, Nutmegger
Delaware = Delawarean
Florida = Floridian
Georgia = Georgian
Hawaii = Hawaiian
Idaho = Idahoan
Illinois = Illinoisan, Illinoisian
Indiana = Indianan, Hoosier
Iowa = Iowan
Kansas = Kansan
Kentucky = Kentuckian
Louisiana = Louisianan, Louisianian
Maine = Mainer, Down Easter
Maryland = Marylander
Massachusetts = Bay Stater, Massachusett
Michigan = Michigander, Michiganian
Minnesota = Minnesotan

Mississippi = Mississippian
Missouri = Missourian
Montana = Montanan
Nebraska = Nebraskan
Nevada = Nevadan
New Hampshire = New Hampshirite
New Jersey = New Jerseyite, New Jerseyan
New Mexico = New Mexican
New York = New Yorker
North Carolina = North Carolinian
North Dakota = North Dakotan
Ohio = Ohioan, Buckeye
Oklahoma = Oklahoman, Oklahomian, Sooner, Okie
Oregon = Oregonian
Pennsylvania = Pennsylvanian
Rhode Island = Rhode Islander
South Carolina = South Carolinian
South Dakota = South Dakotan
Tennessee = Tennesseean
Texas = Texan
Utah = Utahn
Vermont = Vermonter
Virginia = Virginian
Washington = Washingtonian
West Virginia = West Virginian
Wisconsin = Wisconsinite
Wyoming = Wyomingite

Some languages use different demonyms when referring to US Citizens. In Spanish and Portuguese, Latin American speakers will often refer to US Citizens as norteamericanos or norte-americanos.

Colloquial terms such as 'yank' and 'gringo' are also common, with varying levels of negative connotation.

HTML

HyperText Markup Language (HTML) is the computer programming language most used by web browsers to read pages on the internet. It was developed in the 1980's by Tim Berners-Lee and others. There are many additional languages used today to create content on the web, but HTML is still the most common. Here are just a few of the basic codes used to format text in HTML.

`<html>` beginning of an html code
`</html>` end of an html code
`<BR>` line break
`<h1>text</h1>` Heading 1 (2,3,4,5,6) Creates larger, bolded text for a heading to a section.
`<p>text</p>` Creates a paragraph grouping of text
`<b>text</b>` Bolds the text between the tags
`<i>text</i>` Italicizes the text between the tags
`<u>text</u>` Underlines the text between the tags

You can also string attributes together into a single tag group using the font tags.
```
<font size=12 style=bold>Text</font>
```

To create a link to another webpage the code would look something like this.
```
<a href="americanmiscellany.html">Click Here</a>
```

To create a link to an email address you would need a slightly different code such as this.
```
<a href="mailto:me@email.com">Email Me</a>
```

Largest American Cities

According to the US Census Bureau's 2007 population estimates the ten largest cities in the US to have a combined population of 24,931,711 or about 8% of the total population of the United States.

These figures are for the incorporated cities and do not include suburbs or bordering cities that may be included in a Metropolitan Statistical Area.

New York, New York	8,274,527
Los Angeles, California	3,834,340
Chicago, Illinois	2,836,658
Houston, Texas	2,208,180
Phoenix, Arizona	1,552,259
Philadelphia, Pennsylvania	1,449,634
San Antonio, Texas	1,328,984
San Diego, California	1,266,731
Dallas, Texas	1,240,499
San Jose, California	939,899

Cornhusker, NE

When the University of Nebraska Cornhuskers sell out a home game, Memorial Stadium would qualify as the third largest city in Nebraska.

Creepy Crawlies

Insects outnumber people on Earth about 100,000,000 to 1. Let's hope they never realize it.

FOOTBALL POSITIONS

Part of the confusion that many people have with American Football is that there is not a standard set of players and positions on the field at all times. Each team is allowed 11 players on the field, but the positions of these players can vary greatly depending on the situation. Here is a look at a common setup. The positions shown here can be varied to include more receivers in offense, or more defensive backs. In addition to the positions shown, there are also positions known as Special teams. These positions include, Kicker, Holder, Long Snapper, Kick returner, Punt returner, upback, gunner, and in the NFL Punter (usually the kicker punts in college and high school leagues.)

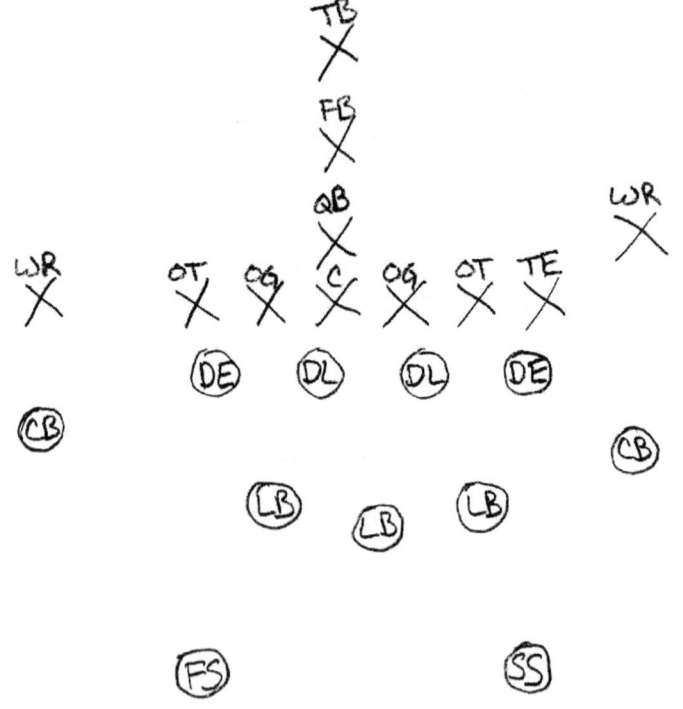

THE EURO

The Euro is the official currency of about 60% of the nations in the European Union. Countries that use the Euro is known as the Eurozone. It was adopted in 1995, was introduced as an accounting currency in 1999 and Euro coins and bills entered circulation in 2002. As of 2009 the Euro has replaced 16 national currencies throughout Europe. Those currencies are listed below with the year they were replaced.

Austrian schilling – 1999
Belgian franc – 1999
Dutch guilder – 1999
Finnish markka – 1999
French franc – 1999
German mark – 1999
Irish pound – 1999
Italian lira – 1999
Luxembourgian franc – 1999
Portuguese escudo – 1999
Spanish peseta – 1999
Greek drachma – 2000
Slovenian tolar – 2006
Cypriot pound – 2007
Maltese lira – 2007
Slovak koruna – 2008

The Euro is also used unofficially by several European states without a currency, including Andorra, Monaco, San Marino, Vatican City, Montenegro, and Kosovo as well as overseas territories of European countries including Mayotte, Saint Pierre and Miquelon, Akrotiri and Dhekalia, Saint Barthélemy and Saint Martin. The Euro is also accepted in the city of Höganas, Sweden along with the Swedish krona.

Road Lines

In the United States different color lines and different patterns in the lines have specific meanings. They can vary from state to state, but generally they follow these meanings.

Dotted Yellow Line - Oncoming traffic, passing allowed.

Solid Yellow Line - Oncoming traffic, no passing.

Dotted White Line - Traffic moving the same direction, passing allowed.

Solid White line - Traffic moving the same direction, no passing or edge of roadway.

Double Lines - When there are two lines next to each other, follow the line closest to you.

Best Preserved Crater

One of the best preserved meteorite craters in the world is the Meteor Crater near Winslow, AZ. Also known as the Barringer Crater, it is 4,150 feet across and 570 feet deep. It is nowhere near the largest known crater on earth, though most craters are not so well preserved because of water, wind, and vegetation. The climate in the Arizona desert has kept the Meteor Crater intact for about 50,000 years.

The largest known impact crater on earth is the Vredefort Crater in South Africa which is 160-190 miles wide.

Can I Have Your Tots?

Tater Tots are more than just he favorite food of every 3-year-old in America. They were invented in 1950's by the Ore-Ida company. The goal was to come up with a product that would use the small bits of potato that were left over when slicing round potatoes into square fries.

They hit store shelves in the mid-1950's and quickly became very popular with children, selling over 60 million pounds every year today. They continue to be a staple in school cafeterias and with certain Idaho teens with awesome nunchucking skills.

What are the Odds?

There has been only one confirmed person hit by a meteorite in all of human history. That person was Ann Hodges of Sylacauga, AL. She was hit by a meteorite that crashed through her roof while she was laying on her sofa in November of 1954. The baseball-sized black rock bounced off a radio and struck her in the thigh, leaving a very large bruise.

A Big Pizza Pie

Americans love their pizza. In fact about 100 acres of pizza are served in the US every day. That's about the size of Vatican City, in pizza. Now that's amore.

COMMON MEDICAL PREFIXES

a- without, not
ab- from, away from
acro- heights, extremities
ad- toward, increase
ambi- both, both sides
an- without, not
ante- before, in front
anti- against
auto- self
bi- two, double
brady- slow
cata- down
circum- around
con- together
contra- against, opposite
de- down, lack of
dia- through, complete
dis- apart, abnormal
dys- difficult, painful
ecto- outside
en- in
endo- within, inner
epi- upon, over
eso- inward
eu- healthy, normal
extra- outside of, beyond
hemi- half
homo- same
hydro- water
hyper- excessive, above
hypo- less than, under
in- in, not

infra- beneath, under
inter- between
intra- within
ipsi- same
juxta- near, beside
macro- large
mal- bad, poor
meso- middle
meta- change, after
micro- small
mono- one, single
multi- many
non- not
nulli- none
pan- all
para- near, beside
per- through
peri- around
poly- many, much
post- after, behind
presby- old age
pro- forward, in front of
pseudo- false
quadri- four
retro- backward, behind
rube- red
sub- under, below
supra- above, over, upward
tachy- rapid, fast
tri- three
ultra- beyond, excess
uni- one

Canadian Holiday's

New Year's Day - January 1st
Good Friday - Friday before Easter
Canada Day - July 1st
Labour Day - First Monday in September
Christmas Day - December 25th

Other Holidays for Most Employers

Though not statutory holidays, these days are recognized by the Federal Government as paid holidays and by many employers. They may be statutory holidays in some provinces and territories.

Easter Monday - Monday after Easter
Victoria Day - Monday on or before May 24th
Thanksgiving - Second Monday in October
Remembrance Day - November 11th
Boxing Day - December 26th

The Name Wendy

Many people think that J.M. Barrie invented the name Wendy for his book, Peter Pan, but that is incorrect. The name dates back hundreds of years before as a shortened form of the Welsh names Gwendolyn and Guinevere. Ironically Wendy was originally a masculine name. Barrie did have a great effect on the popularity of the name and solidifying it as a female name.

Rockall

Rockall is a 56 foot rock located in the North Atlantic Ocean. It has been known to sailors since at least the 16th Century. Officially it is part of the Outer Hebrides of Scotland and is therefore considered part of the UK, which claims territorial waters surrounding the rock. Only about 20 people are confirmed to have actually set foot on the rock, fewer than have walked on the Moon. It is located at 57°35'46.695" N 13°41'14.308" W.

The Doctors (Who)

The popular BBC series Doctor Who has been around for over 50 years now (not continuously). The revived series has brought whole new generations into a fandom that was already widespread in Britain. There have been 12 actors to play the title character (The Doctor) and one more that played a regeneration that was not known as The Doctor. Here is a list of those actors and their respective time as The Doctor.

First	William Hartnell (1963-1966)
Second	Patrick Troughton (1966-1969)
Third	Jon Pertwee (1970-1974)
Fourth	Tom Baker (1974-1980)
Fifth	Peter Davison (1981-1984)
Sixth	Colin Baker (1984-1986)
Seventh	Sylvester McCoy (1987-1989)
Eighth	Paul McGann (1996)
War Doctor	John Hurt (2013)
Ninth	Christopher Eccleston (2005)
Tenth	David Tennant (2005-2010)
Eleventh	Matt Smith (2010-2013)
Twelfth	Peter Capaldi (2013-)

CREDIT CARD NUMBERS

Most credit/debit card numbers in the US are 16 digits and all have the same basic structure. This is because of the ANSI Standard X4.13-1983. This is the industry standard for Financial Transaction Cards set out by the American National Standards Institute in 1983. Here are some of the general rules about card numbers.

First Digit - Signifies the type of card.
3 - Travel/Entertainment Cards (American Express, Diners Club, etc.)
4 - Banking/Financial (Visa)
5 - Banking/Financial (Mastercard)
6 - Merchandising/Banking (Discover)

First 6 Digits - Is the Issuer Identifier Number. This signifies who issued the card and what kind of card it is (ie platinum, gold, Walmart Prepaid, etc.)

After the first 6 digits is the Account Number. This can be up to 12 digits, but most issuers today use 9 digit account numbers.

The final digit of the card number is a check digit. This validates the number using the Luhn algorithm, making just randomly making up a valid card number very remote.

TEXAN TIGERS

There are more tigers in captivity in Texas than there are in the wild worldwide.

WHERE THE BUFFALO ROAM

American Buffalo or Bison once had a range that
extended from the Canadian Northwest Territories in
the North, to the Mexican states of Durango and Nuevo
León in the South and from Pennsylvania and Virginia
in the East to Idaho and Nevada in the West.

Their numbers were once in the millions, but they
were hunted to within a few hundred animals by the
late 19th Century. Today they number in the hundreds
of thousands and there are both wild and domestic
herds throughout North America as well as animals in
captivity around the world.

FAMOUS MUSTACHES

Tom Selleck
Albert Einstein
Teddy Roosevelt
Kaiser Wilhelm
Jeff Foxworthy
Adolph Hitler
Saddam Hussein
Sonny Bono
Yosemite Sam
Hulk Hogan
Charlie Chaplan
William Howard Taft
Mike Ditka
Ned Flanders
Groucho Marx
Wyatt Earp

Rocks

There are three basic types of rocks, igneous, sedimentary, and metamorphic. These groups are subdivided into many other groups. The study of rocks is called petrology, which is a part of geology (the study of the earth). Below are some examples of specific rocks in each group.

Igneous
granite
pumice
basalt
obsidian

Sedimentary
sandstone
shale
limestone
conglomerate

Metamorphic
marble
gneiss
slate
schist

Negative Calories in Celery?

An average 8 inch stalk of celery contains about 6 calories. Digesting the celery will take more than 6 calories, meaning that celery actually has negative calories overall. Though the difference is so small you could eat celery all day and not make much difference.

Men Who Walked on the Moon

There are only 12 men who have walked on the moon. They all walked between 1969 and 1972. Only the United States has managed to land people to moon and safely home again.

Neil Armstrong, Apollo 11
Buzz Aldrin, Apollo 11
Pete Conran, Apollo 12
Alan Bean, Apollo 12
Alan Shepard, Apollo 14
Edgar Mitchell, Apollo 14
David Scott, Apollo 15
James Irwin, Apollo 15
John W. Young, Apollo 16
Charles Duke, Apollo 16
Eugene Cernan, Apollo 17
Harrison Schmitt, Apollo 17

Jim Lovell and Fred Haise were scheduled to land on the moon in 1970 as part of the Apollo 13 mission, but were forced to abort the attempt after an oxygen tank ruptured two days into the 16 day mission.

Chocolate

Who doesn't love chocolate? In fact we love it so much that over 8,600,000 pounds of chocolate are consumed every day… that's about 100 pounds a second.

You Are What You Eat

Five species of grass account for half the calories in the human diet. Grains are all part of the grass family.

London Bridge in Arizona

The 19th Century London Bridge that was built in the 1920's spanning the Thames River in London was dismantled in 1967 to make way for a new bridge. The old bridge was sold to American businessman Robert McCulloch for $1.2 Million. He had the bridge dismantled and then re-assembled as a façade on a new bridge in Lake Havesu, AZ.

'Ōlelo Hawai'i

Hawaiian alphabet has only 13 letters. Written Hawaiian has been around since 1822 when it had 22 letters, but there have been some changes to the way it was written over the years. The written language was simplified to better represent the actual sounds of the Hawaiian language. The current alphabet used is similar to most written polynesian languages today. It includes 5 vowels A, E, I, O, U and 8 consonants; H, K, L, M, N, P, W and 'okina, which is represented by an apostrophe ('). Each vowel can be either long or short. Long vowels are sometimes (but not always) written with a macron over them to indicate that it is long (Ā, Ē, Ī, Ō, Ū).

That's Not a Knot

Technically speaking, a 'knot' uses only a single line. To join two lines or ropes together you use a 'bend' and to attach a line to a pole or other structure you would use a 'hitch.' So a square knot is neither square nor a knot.

DR. SUESS BOOKS

Thomas Suess Giesel, who wrote under the pen name of Dr. Suess, is one of the most prolific and well known children's authors and illustrators in America. He wrote and illustrated 48 books between 1937 and his death in 1990. He also wrote other books under the name Theo. LeSieg. Here is listed all of the books he wrote and illustrated under the name, Dr. Suess.

And to Think That I Saw It on Mulberry Street - 1937
The 500 Hats of Bartholomew Cubbins - 1938
The King's Stilts - 1939
The Seven Lady Godivas - 1939
Horton Hatches the Egg - 1940
McElligot's Pool - 1947
Thidwick the Big-Hearted Moose - 1948
Bartholomew and the Oobleck - 1949
If I Ran the Zoo - 1950
Scrambled Eggs Super! - 1953
Horton Hears a Who! - 1954
On Beyond Zebra! - 1955
If I Ran the Circus - 1956
How the Grinch Stole Christmas! - 1957
The Cat in the Hat - 1957
The Cat in the Hat Comes Back - 1958
Yertle the Turtle and Other Stories - 1958
Happy Birthday to You! - 1959
One Fish Two Fish Red Fish Blue Fish - 1960
Green Eggs and Ham - 1960
The Sneetches and Other Stories - 1961
Dr. Seuss's Sleep Book - 1962

Dr. Seuss's ABC: An Amazing Alphabet Book! - 1963
Hop on Pop - 1963
Fox in Socks - 1965
I Had Trouble in Getting to Solla Sollew - 1965
The Cat in the Hat Song Book - 1967
The Foot Book - 1968
I Can Lick 30 Tigers Today! and Other Stories - 1969
My Book about ME - 1970
I Can Draw It Myself - 1970
Mr. Brown Can Moo! Can You?: Dr. Seuss's Book of
Wonderful Noises! - 1970
The Lorax - 1971
Marvin K. Mooney Will You Please Go Now! - 1972
Did I Ever Tell You How Lucky You Are? - 1973
The Shape of Me and Other Stuff - 1973
There's a Wocket in My Pocket! - 1974
Great Day for Up! - 1974
Oh, the Thinks You Can Think! - 1975
The Cat's Quizzer - 1976
I Can Read with My Eyes Shut! - 1978
Oh Say Can You Say? - 1979
Hunches in Bunches - 1982
The Butter Battle Book - 1984
You're Only Old Once!: A Book for Obsolete Children-1986
I Am NOT Going to Get Up Today! - 1987
Oh, the Places You'll Go! - 1990

During his lifetime, many of Dr. Suess' stories
were made into cartoons, including the famous 1966
adaptation of *How the Grinch Stole Christmas*. Since his
death, several have been made into feature length films,
both live-action and computer animated, with varying
success.

Military Ranks/Rates (Enlisted)

	Army	Navy/ Coast Guard	Marine Corps	Air Force
E-1	Private	Seaman Recruit	Private	Airman Basic
E-2	PV2	SA	PFC	Amn
E-3	PFC	SN	LCpl	A1C
E-4	CPL SPC	PO3	Cpl	SrA
E-5	SGT	PO2	Sgt	SSgt
E-6	SSG	PO1	SSgt	TSgt
E-7	SFC	CPO	GySgt	MSgt 1Sgt
E-8	MSG 1SG	SCPO	MSgt 1Sgt	SMSgt 1SMSgt
E-9	SGM CSM	MCPO CMCPO	MGySgt SgtMaj	CMSgt 1CMSgt CCMSgt
E-9	SMA	MCPON / MCPOCG	SgtMajMC	CMSAF

MILITARY RANKS (OFFICER)

	ARMY	NAVY/ COAST GUARD	MARINE CORPS	AIR FORCE

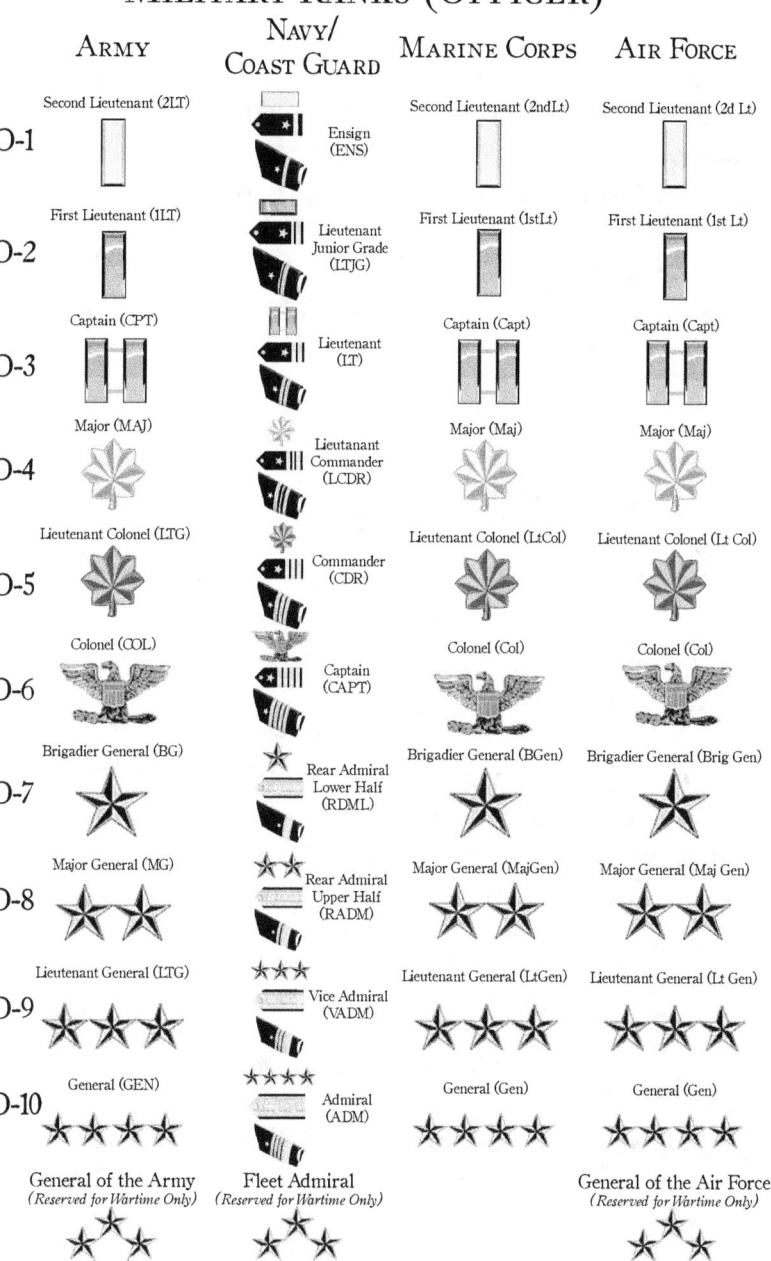

O-1 — Second Lieutenant (2LT) — Ensign (ENS) — Second Lieutenant (2ndLt) — Second Lieutenant (2d Lt)

O-2 — First Lieutenant (1LT) — Lieutenant Junior Grade (LTJG) — First Lieutenant (1stLt) — First Lieutenant (1st Lt)

O-3 — Captain (CPT) — Lieutenant (LT) — Captain (Capt) — Captain (Capt)

O-4 — Major (MAJ) — Lieutenant Commander (LCDR) — Major (Maj) — Major (Maj)

O-5 — Lieutenant Colonel (LTG) — Commander (CDR) — Lieutenant Colonel (LtCol) — Lieutenant Colonel (Lt Col)

O-6 — Colonel (COL) — Captain (CAPT) — Colonel (Col) — Colonel (Col)

O-7 — Brigadier General (BG) — Rear Admiral Lower Half (RDML) — Brigadier General (BGen) — Brigadier General (Brig Gen)

O-8 — Major General (MG) — Rear Admiral Upper Half (RADM) — Major General (MajGen) — Major General (Maj Gen)

O-9 — Lieutenant General (LTG) — Vice Admiral (VADM) — Lieutenant General (LtGen) — Lieutenant General (Lt Gen)

O-10 — General (GEN) — Admiral (ADM) — General (Gen) — General (Gen)

General of the Army *(Reserved for Wartime Only)* — Fleet Admiral *(Reserved for Wartime Only)* — General of the Air Force *(Reserved for Wartime Only)*

The Flag of Tennessee

Tennessee's flag is original and has a lot of symbolism. The three stars represent the mountains, highlands, and lowlands of the state. The three regions are held together with the unbroken circle, representing unity. The flag is red, with a blue background inside the circle. There is also a band of blue on the end of the flag to keep the flag from appearing plain red when it is limp.

Lincoln's Beard

Abraham Lincoln's beard was the suggestion of 11 year old Grace Bedell of Westfield, NY who wrote to Lincoln while he was running for President on October 15, 1960, telling him in part, "All the ladies like whiskers and they would tease their husband's to vote for you and then you would be President."

Lincoln replied to her letter on October 19, 1860 saying, "As to the whiskers, having never worn any, do you not think people would call it a piece of silly affection if I were to begin it now?" By the time he left Springfield for his inauguration on February 11, 1861 he had his trademark beard.

Press Start to Begin

If you were an arcade ace in the '80's you might dream of getting a perfect score in Pacman, which is 3,333,360 points for some reason.

Isaac Asimov

Issac Asimov published books in nine of the 10 major categories found in the Dewey-Decimal System. He did not publish a book in the 100's, Philosophy and Psychology. He did publish books in each of the other categories:

000, Computer Science, Information & General Works
200, Religion
300, Social Sciences
400, Language
500, Science (including Mathematics)
600, Technology
700, Arts and Recreation
800, Literature
900, History, Geography and Biography

Asimov published over 500 titles over 53 years of his life. He is considered one of the most prolific writers of all time.

Lowest High and the Highest Low

The state with the lowest highest point is Florida. Britton hill is only 345 ft (105 m) above sea level.

The state with the highest low point is Colorado, whose lowest point is the Arikaree River and the Kansas border at 3317 ft (1011 m) above sea level.

This means you would have to dig down 2972 ft (905 m) at the lowest point in Colorado to reach the highest point in Florida.

THE HOKEY POKEY

There are a lot of stories as to the origin of this song and the accompanying dance. It is sure that Ray Anthony recorded the most popular version in the 1950's. The words and accompanying actions usually go like this...

You put your right arm in.
You put your right arm out.
You put your right arm in, and you shake it all about.
You do the Hokey Pokey and you turn yourself around.
That's what it's all about!

You continue with various body parts (left arm, right leg, head, etc.) usually ending with your "whole self."

The song then ends with...

You do the Hokey Pokey!
You do the Hokey Pokey!
You do the Hokey Pokey!
That's what it's all about!

KILLER DOLPHINS

Killer Whales are actually a species of dolphin (the confusion stems from the Spanish, who called them 'whale killers'). Unlike most whales, they're gregarious, have teeth and eat large animals (including whales) rather than krill or plankton. The Romans called them orcas ("demons from Hell" in Latin).

Provinces of Canada

There are 10 Provinces and three territories that make up Canada. They are:

Province- Capital
Ontario - Toronto
Quebec - Quebec City
Nova Scotia - Halifax
New Brunswick - Fredericton
Manitoba - Winnipeg
British Columbia - Victoria
Prince Edward Island - Charlottetown
Saskatchewan - Regina
Alberta - Edmonton
Newfoundland and Labrador - St. John's

Territory- Capital
Northwest Territories - Yellowknife
Yukon - Whitehorse
Nunavut – Iqaluit

Pilgrim's Pride

About 10% of Americans today (approximately 35 million) can trace their roots back to one of the 102 people that sailed on the Mayflower in 1620.

Big Kitty-Fish

The European Wels catfish can grow to sizes up to 16 feet long and weigh over 800 lbs. This makes it the largest freshwater fish found naturally in Europe. There are even theories that the Loch Ness Monster is really a giant catfish.

Smell After It Rains

There are many things that can cause a distinctive smell after it rains, but one of the most common smells after it rains is caused by the bacteria Actinomycetes. This bacteria thrives in moist warm ground, but when the ground dries out it releases spores and when it rains these spores are spread into the air where they have a distinctive smell. A smell after rain can also be caused by the acidity of the rainwater or also by the oils from trees and other plants that can collect on the surface of rocks and other surfaces reacting with the rain.

Holy Catchphrases Batman!

A total of 352 "Holy _____" phrases were used by Burt Ward as Robin on the 1960's Batman TV series. They ranged from "Holy Agility, Batman" to "Holy Zorro".

Television Ratings

Television ratings by Neilson Media Research include two different numbers, gross rating points and share.

A rating point is a percent of all households that have a television. In 2010 Neilson estimated there were 115.9 Million television households in the United States. Each rating point represents about 1,159,000 households.

A share is a percent of the television audience at that time. So, while a rating point counts every household that has a television, share only counts those households that are watching television at that time. Because of this, share is always higher than gross rating.

Computer Prefixes

There can be a lot of confusion when it comes to computer systems and their use of various prefixes to represent memory. There are two systems used to represent data space in computers which usually use the same set of prefixes, making it even more confusing. Below is a table explaining the value of various terms.

bit(b) = one digit of binary code (a 1 or a 0)
byte(B) = one character in binary code (8 bits)
nibble or nyble = half a binary character (4 bits)

Prefix	Binary Value
Kilo (K)	2^{10} = 1,024
Mega (M)	2^{20} = 1,048,576
Giga (G)	2^{30} = 1,073,741,824
Tera (T)	2^{40} = 1,099,511,627,776
Peta (P)	2^{50} = 1,125,899,906,842,624
Exa (E)	2^{60} = 1,152,921,504,606,846,976
Zetta (Z)	2^{70} = 1,180,591,620,717,411,303,424
Yotta (Y)	2^{80} = 1,208,925,819,614,629,174,706,176

Prefix	Decimal Value
Kilo (K)	10^{3} - 1,000
Mega (M)	10^{6} - 1,000,000
Giga (G)	10^{9} - 1,000,000,000
Tera (T)	10^{12} - 1,000,000,000,000
Peta (P)	10^{15} - 1,000,000,000,000,000
Exa (E)	10^{18} - 1,000,000,000,000,000,000
Zetta (Z)	10^{21} - 1,000,000,000,000,000,000,000
Yotta (Y)	10^{24} - 1,000,000,000,000,000,000,000,000

States of Mexico

State - Capital City - Postal Abbreviation
Aguascalientes - Aguascalientes - AGU
Baja California - Mexicali - BCN
Baja California Sur - La Paz - BCS
Campeche - Campeche - CAM
Chiapas - Tuxtla Gutiérrez - CHP
Chihuahua - Chihuahua - CHH
Coahuila - Saltillo - COA
Colima - Colima - COL
Durango - Durango - DUR
Guanajuato - Guanajuato - GUA
Guerrero - Chilpancingo - GRO
Hidalgo - Pachuca - HID
Jalisco - Guadalajara - JAL
Mexico State - Toluca - MEX
Michoacán - Morelia - MIC
Morelos - Cuernavaca - MOR
Nayarit - Tepic - NAY
Nuevo León - Monterrey - NLE
Oaxaca - Oaxaca - OAX
Puebla - Puebla - PUE
Querétaro - Querétaro - QUE
Quintana Roo - Chetumal - ROO
San Luis Potosí - San Luis Potosí - SLP
Sinaloa - Culiacán - SIN
Sonora - Hermosillo - SON
Tabasco - Villahermosa - TAB
Tamaulipas - Ciudad Victoria - TAM
Tlaxcala - Tlaxcala - TLA
Veracruz - Xalapa - VER
Yucatán - Mérida - YUC
Zacatecas - Zacatecas - ZAC

THE LARGEST CITY IN UNITED STATES

The "largest" city by area in the United States is Juneau, Alaska. It covers about 3,000 square miles. That's larger than the State of Delaware. In case you are wondering, Jacksonville, Florida is the largest in the lower 48 at just over 800 square miles.

ARLINGTON

Gen. Robert E. Lee married a relative of George Washington, Mary Ann Randolph Custis. She owned a plantation called "Arlington." They lived there 30 years until Gen. Lee resigned his commission to avoid fighting against his home state. The Lees vacated the property in 1861. Union troops occupied it during the Civil War and 200 acres were set aside to bury fallen Union soldiers. Today over 250,000 war dead from every conflict since the Civil War are buried there. Now, of course, it is known as Arlington National Cemetery.

AS AMERICAN AS TUMBLEWEEDS

The classic tumbleweed is a symbol of the American West and can still be found in large numbers all across North and South America. The funny thing here is that the tumbleweed is an invasive species. Most "tumbleweeds" are actually the Russian Thistle *Kali Tragus*. It was introduced to South Dakota in the 1800's and has since spread from Canada to Chile.

Balloon Bombs

During World War II Japan sent incendiary bombs to the United States mainland using weather balloons. It was a very far-fetched plan that might have worked, had 1944 not been a very wet year in the Pacific Northwest. A family in Oregon was actually killed when one such bomb fell on their house. That is, however, the only fatalities from the program, which was scrapped shortly after it started.

Half of What You Know

Studies of the frequency of citations of scientific papers show they become obsolete at a predictable rate. Harvard mathematician Samuel Arbesman calls this "the half-life of facts." Just as with radioactive decay, you can't tell when any one "fact" will reach its expiry date, but you can predict how long it will take for half the facts in any discipline to do so. In medicine, for example, "truth" seems to have a 45-year half-life. Some medical schools teach students that, within a few years, half of what they've been taught will be wrong – they just don't know which half. In mathematics, the rate of decay is much slower. Very few accepted mathematical proofs get disproved.

McLove

Approximately 1 in 8 workers in America have been employed by McDonald's at some point, including the author of this book.

Air Quality Index "AQI"

Each category corresponds to a different level of health concern. The six levels of health concern and what they mean are:

"Good" AQI is 0 - 50. Air quality is considered satisfactory, and air pollution poses little or no risk.

"Moderate" AQI is 51 - 100. Air quality is acceptable; however, for some pollutants there may be a moderate health concern for a very small number of people. For example, people who are unusually sensitive to ozone may experience respiratory symptoms.

"Unhealthy for Sensitive Groups" AQI is 101 - 150. Although general public is not likely to be affected at this AQI range, people with lung disease, older adults and children are at a greater risk from exposure to ozone, whereas persons with heart and lung disease, older adults and children are at greater risk from the presence of particles in the air. .

"Unhealthy" AQI is 151 - 200. Everyone may begin to experience some adverse health effects, and members of the sensitive groups may experience more serious effects. .

"Very Unhealthy" AQI is 201 - 300. This would trigger a health alert signifying that everyone may experience more serious health effects.

"Hazardous" AQI greater than 300. This would trigger a health warnings of emergency conditions. The entire population is more likely to be affected.

Waffle House Index

The Federal Emergency Management Agency (FEMA) uses an informal scale called the "Waffle House Index" to help determine the level of impact a storm has on an area, particularly in the southern United States. The scale was developed because of the Waffle House's reputation for staying open, even in harsh circumstances. FEMA Head Craig Fugate was quoted saying "If you get there and the Waffle House is closed, that's really bad" The scale has three color coded levels, explained below.

GREEN - Restaurant is open with normal operations and full menu.
YELLOW - Restaurant is only serving a limited menu, may not have full utilities (power, running water).
RED - Restaurant is closed, indicating severe damage, unable to operate in any capacity.

The index very rarely reaches the red level.

The Pizza Principle

The price of a slice of pizza in New York City has been approximately equal to the cost of a subway ride for the past 50 years.

That's a Butt Load of Knowledge

A Butt is an actual unit of measure. In the middle ages a butt was equal to two hogsheads or about 126 gallons.

A Billion and a Million

One billion is a million times larger than one million. In perspective, a million seconds is just over 11 days. A billion seconds is over 31 years. (Unless you live in Britain, where a billion is even larger.)

Female Special Agents

The first female FBI Special Agents were Susan Roley Malone, a former Marine and Joanne Pierce Misko, a former Catholic Nun. They both became Special Agents as part of the first FBI Training Academy class to accept women in 1972.

Northern Lights

The Northern Lights, or *aurora borealis*, are caused by charged particles colliding in the upper atmosphere (thermosphere). The particles come from the solar wind and are directed toward the poles by the Earth's magnetic field. The lights' color depends on the type of particles and how they are interacting. Colors are usually green and yellow, but can sometimes be blue and red. While the aurora is usually only seen at very high latitudes, during geomagnetic storms it can be seen at lower latitudes. There are also Southern Lights, the *aurora australis*, the same phenomenon near the southern pole.

Press 1 For English

Though English is the most commonly spoken language in the United States, there is no official language.

CRAZY AMERICAN TRADITIONS

Let's face it, Americans have some pretty crazy traditions. While we may not roll cheese, throw tomatoes or run with bulls, we have our own way of doing some pretty nutty things to celebrate stuff that no one else finds celebratory. Here are just a few of them.

TAILGATING - Before you go inside a stadium for a major football game (college or pro) many people bring grills and cook out in the parking lot. They share food, drinks and have a party right there on the tailgate of their trucks (hence the name). Today, a truck is not required to tailgate and some people will tailgate even when they don't have tickets to go inside the game, they just watch it on TV from the parking lot.

SUPERBOWL COMMERCIALS - Only in America can commercials become a tradition. The biggest sporting event of the year is also the highest rated program on television (most years). Because of this the price of a 30 second ad has been climbing steadily for over 40 years. And if you are going to spend $4 Million to air a commercial you might as well put a bit more effort to make it a pretty good one. With that we get football playing horses, talking frogs, cat-herders, Mean Joe Green being nice and Betty White getting tackled. Let's be honest, most of the time the commercials are better than the game, right?

TRICK OR TREATING - Most societies would shun going door to door begging for candy (or is it threatening for candy?). While many areas now host "Trunk or Treat" events that try to replicate the experience from the trunk of a car in a parking lot, there is something fun about decorating your home to scare children that is lost when you don't have the home field advantage.

TURKEY PARDONS - Every President since Truman has received a Thanksgiving turkey from various groups (usually the National Turkey Federation). In the early days many of those birds were actually eaten, Truman indicated that he ate at least a few of the birds he was presented. Ronald Reagan first "pardoned" a turkey in 1987, as a bit of a joke for the press. His successor, George H.W. Bush made it an annual event and usually one or two turkeys are presented to the President and he grants them a "Presidential Pardon" after which they spend the rest of their lives at a petting zoo. Turkeys raised for meat do not normally have a long life and many of the birds are dead within a year.

BLACK FRIDAY - Shopping could be termed our national pastime, but that is likely to make some baseball fans upset. The day after Thanksgiving Day is seen as the beginning of the holiday shopping season that stretches from Thanksgiving to Christmas (or New Year's Day). While Black Friday get's all the attention with its deals and ever-earlier opening times (some on Thanksgiving Day now) it actually has only been the busiest shopping day of the year consistently since 2005. Some years the busiest day is actually closer to Christmas Day.

CRAZY AMERICAN TRADITIONS (CONTINUED)

GROUNDHOG DAY - While weather people are not known for the accuracy of their predictions, why you would want to trust your prediction to a large member of the squirrel family I'm not sure. The tradition goes that if the groundhog sees his shadow on February 2nd, then there will be six more weeks of winter weather. If it is cloudy and the groundhog doesn't see its shadow then spring will come early. The largest Groundhog Day celebration is in Punxsutawney, PA with the groundhog Punxsutawney Phil.

STANDARD MEASURES - Based on the British Imperial Measures system, the US standard system of weights and measures has persisted despite numerous attempts to bring the more global Metric System (SI) into daily use. While metric units may be used in some commerce (like some soda bottles) and is widely accepted in scientific and medical fields, "standard" measures are still more common overall.

COCKROACHES AND RADIATION

The myth that cockroaches can survive a nuclear blast is commonly believed, but no one quite knows where it comes from. While the common cockroach would survive much more radiation exposure than a human (about 10,000 rads vs. our 1000 rads) they are not even close to the record for insects or living organisms. There are insects that research indicate could survive levels up to 180,000 rads of radiation and certain bacteria could survive between 1.5 and 3 Million rads! Let's hope some super-villain never gives us the chance to test these levels.

Is Ohio the 17th State or 47th?

There are many who point to the strange way that Ohio became a state. Since it was pretty early in the whole "state-making" period of the country there weren't hard and fast set rules for making a state. The previous three states added (Vermont, Tennessee and Kentucky) were all created from territory that already belonged to another state, or was disputed by two different states. Ohio was created from the Northwest Territories and the wording of the bill that went through congress was different than what was used to create most states after that time. When the 150th anniversary of statehood was coming up, some believed that Ohio had never been officially admitted to the Union because there was no act of Congress designating it so. To clear the matter up quickly Congress passed a bill in 1953 retroactively creating Ohio on March 1, 1803. Later legal and constitutional scholars believe that the measure was actually unnecessary, as the original bill organizing the State said that Ohio would be admitted to the Union as soon as the state government was organized. The Ohio State Legislature officially convened for the first time on March 1, 1803, so either way the date is the same, making Ohio the 17th State.

Live Longer Than a Goldfish

It wasn't until 1920 that a newborn infant in the United States had an expected life expectancy longer than a goldfish's. In 1919 the life expectance was only 48.4 years. Many species of wild goldfish live for over 50 years.

Bumblebees Can Fly?

These comically proportioned insects can be a source of glee but with fat fuzzy bodies it doesn't seem like they should be able to fly. In fact many people claim that scientists don't know how they fly. This is of course incorrect and most likely originated from a few sources in the early 20th Century that claimed that according to the laws of aerodynamics they shouldn't be able to fly, which was true at the time. In the past hundred years science has come to understand the laws of flight much better and it is no mystery how bumblebees fly. In fact, scientists can even recreate the flight method of a bee with a very tiny robot. And you thought drones were a problem. Why is there a tiny red light flashing on that bee?

Funeral for a Fly

The Roman poet Virgil once held a funeral for his pet housefly. It included a guest list that included many of the wealthy and powerful of the city. A long eulogy was delivered and a tomb was erected for the fly on the grounds of Virgil's house. While poets can be known for being eccentric, this was likely not just your average "winning" meltdown. The Second Triumverate had recently defeated Julius Caesar's assassins at the battle of Phillipi. They were then seizing the property of the rich and distributing it to the war veterans as payment. The only exception they made was if the estate housed a burial tomb. So, by burying his pet housefly, Virgil saved his house. I'd loved to have been a fly on the wall when he came up with that scheme... or maybe not actually.

No license Plates

Everyone knows that you have to register your car with the state you live in and display license plates on it. Steve Jobs, the late Apple CEO didn't have license plates on his car thanks to a loophole and a large budget. According to California Law the owner of a new car had 6 months to register their vehicle and display a license plate. Jobs got around this by simply getting a new car every 6 months, therefore never violating the rule. The law has since been amended to shorten that time frame to 3 months. If you don't mind buying a new car all the time, you might get away with having no licence plate. (Though it is probably easier to just get the plates.)

Everything is a Lie!

A day on Earth is not the 24 hours you've always been told. A day is actually 23 hours, 56 minutes and 4.1 seconds long. Lies, all lies!

Space Pen

The story of the space pen is a classic tale of out of control government spending. It is also completely false. First, pencils in space are actually dangerous because they can break off, leaving little projectiles floating around to get lodged in equipment or even inhaled. Second they are also flammable, which is something that just isn't a good idea in space (you've seen that episode of Firefly with the fire right?). The space pen was a real necessity that was developed by the Fisher Pen Company, funded completely with their own money. NASA then bought the pens for a whopping $6 each. Within a few years of their introduction, even the Soviets were buying them.

Index

INDEX

INDEX

INDEX

INDEX

INDEX

INDEX

ABOUT THE AUTHOR

Michael A. Cousin is a marketing professional and collector of useless information. He has loved trivia and reading about random things since he was a kid. He was even voted "Most likely to host a game show" by his high school class. Michael lives in Idaho Falls, ID with his wife, Stephanie and their three children.